Not While
I have Ammo

TO BAILEY

BEST WISHS

Jim

Not While I have Ammo

A History of Captain Connie Mackey, Defender of the Strand

JIM CORBETT

NONSUCH

*This book is dedicated to the memory of
my grandfather, Connie McNamara, and also
to my mother, Patsy Corbett.*

First published 2008

Nonsuch Publishing
73 Lower Leeson Street
Dublin 2, Ireland
www.thehistorypress.co.uk

Nonsuch Publishing is an imprint of The History Press

British Library Cataloguing in Publication Data.
A catalogue record for this book is available from the British Library.

ISBN 978 1 84588 916 6

Typesetting and origination by The History Press
Printed in Great Britain by Ashford Colour Press Ltd, Gosport, Hampshire

Contents

Captain Connie Mackey
6 April 1896 − 15 December 1957
'A' Company, Second Battalion,
Mid-Limerick Brigade,
Irish Volunteers 1916 − 1923.

Foreword

When Connie 'Mackey' McNamara died in 1957 he left behind a legacy which was in great danger of being consigned to the realms of the forgotten. He was not a man who extolled his own virtues, and so what Connie had achieved was in great danger of being lost. Fortunately for his descendants, and indeed for all who have an interest in the past, his grandson Jim Corbett took on the research of Connie McNamara, his times and his adventures. Jim never met his grandfather, having been born long after Connie had died, but from the research he has carried out, he has, effectively, brought Connie back to life. His painstaking research has breathed new life into a man who was born at the end of the nineteenth century and lived through some of the most momentous times in Irish history.

Connie McNamara was born into a Limerick far removed from that of the vibrant city of the twenty-first century. It was an inward-looking place, whose industrial life was dominated by the activities of four big bacon factories; Shaw's (which later became Clover Meats in 1950), Matterson's, O'Mara's and Denny's, and the milk processing plant belonging to the Cleeve family. The owners of these big factories were largely members of a Protestant commercial class which had little in common with their largely Catholic workforce. When Connie McNamara joined the IRA in 1916 he was setting out on a treacherous road, and few could have predicted where it would lead. Unlike some of those who joined up, Connie McNamara was not simply going through the motions, and he soon began to rise through the ranks of the IRA. He took part in a number of actions in the War of Independence, the most notable of which being the rescue of Robert Byrne from the Union Hospital in April 1919. Unfortunately Byrne died as a result of wounds received from one of his RIC guards, Constable Spillane, making him the first Republican casualty of the war.

Following the signing of the Treaty in December 1921, Connie McNamara took the Anti-Treaty side. As the Civil War broke out in Limerick in July 1922, Connie was in charge of the garrison of the Strand Barracks. When the barracks was shelled by Free State artillery, Connie and his comrades resisted bravely, but eventually, when the barracks was in ruins, they were forced to surrender. He was complimented for his bravery and tenacity by the officer in charge of the attacking force. Following the surrender Connie was imprisoned along with a number of very important national figures.

His standing was such that when he applied for a pension in later years, among his referees was Michael Brennan, who was in charge of the Free State forces in the Limerick area. This is very significant, as, more than anything, it reflects Connie's standing not just among his comrades and friends, but even among those who were later his enemies.

Tom Toomey, M.A.

Tom Toomey is a local Limerick historian. He co-authored *An Antique and Storied Land: A History of the Parish of Donoughmore, Knockea, Roxborough and its Environs in County Limerick* with H. Greensmyth in 1991. In 1995 he published *Forgotten Dreams: The life and times of Major J.G. 'Ged' O'Dwyer*. He has also written numerous local history articles for various publications. He is currently working on a history of Limerick during the Irish Independence struggle, 1912-1921.

Acknowledgements

In writing this history of Cornelius McNamara, there were a number of people who were incredibly generous, and I would like to thank them for their assistance and patience in dealing with my often difficult requests and never-ending enquiries in the search for nuggets of information relating to my grandfather, and the period covered. Without their support and encouragement, I would have been unable to compile this history and see my dream realised.

A very sincere and genuine thank you to the following: Roger Black and the staff of the Roger Black Gallery, who arranged to have the black and white picture of Connie in his Volunteer uniform painted; Commandants Liam Campbell and Victor Laing, of Military Archives, Cathal Brugha Barracks, who pointed me in the right direction and gave my research focus; Marie Treacy and Margret Kilcommins, of the Veterans Administration section, Department of Defence, in Renmore, Galway, who provided Connie's pension details, which included a statement of his military service; Lar Joye, of the National Museum, Collins Barracks, Dublin, who allowed me to photograph Volunteer uniforms and translated the Gormanstown Choir names into English from Irish; Deirdre Griffin of Limerick City Registrars, St Camillus' Hospital, Limerick, for the birth, marriage and death certificates of the McNamara, Moakley and Corbett families, which allowed me to build a family tree; Sharon Clancy, who kindly obtained a copy of Connie's obituary; Des Long, of the Limerick Republican Graves Association, who provided me with

IRA membership lists; Tom Toomey, for clarifying various Volunteer activities and allowing me to get into a Volunteer's mindset; Phillip Turner, for drawing the map of the Strand Barracks; Mike Ratcliffe of Snappy Snaps, Croydon, for his advice in illustrating the book; James McMahon and Roger Boulter, for allowing me access to their research; Gearóid Moroney for setting up the website: www.conniemackey.com; John O'Shaughnessy and Tom O'Neill for their sympathetic editing and proofreading – they made an unruly work look respectable.

And last but not least, thank you to the various members of the Corbett, McNamara and Moakley families, whose first-hand information and family records were invaluable, and to the many other people whose kind assistance helped me to produce this book. I apologise to anyone I have left out. Any errors or omissions are entirely my own, my sincerest thanks to you all.

About the Author

Jim Corbett was born and educated in Limerick City. He left Limerick after secondary school and moved to Croydon, England in 1988, where he still lives. He briefly studied business in London and has spent the past twelve years working in the telecommunications industry in London. While working for Vodafone, he wrote the Vodafone Music Club Weekly Magazine. He began writing in 2005 and is very much interested in twentieth-century Irish history.

Preface

I am Connie's grandson. All through my life my mother told me stories about my grandfather Cornelius McNamara, a member of the Old IRA. We had his War of Independence Medal, a picture, and an old bullet from a battle that took place in the Strand Barracks, Limerick, during the Irish Civil War. Also in our possession was an autograph book, with some strange illustrations and poems from his time as a prisoner of war at Gormanstown Internment Camp, Co. Meath. My mother told me stories about her father; of fellow Volunteers he was interned with, of being forced to run over broken glass, and of having to sleep in graveyards when he was on the run from the British. But apart from that, we never knew the full background of our grandfather, who, as it transpired, had a fascinating story to tell.

I decided to find out as much as I could about this amazing man, whom I had never met. As I researched his contribution to Irish history, I had a growing desire to have his life documented for posterity. He was one of a golden generation of unselfish Irishmen with high ideals who were prepared to risk and endure everything for the sake of their country and countrymen. I wanted to give him the place in history that I felt he deserved, and to give back to the people of Limerick, the story of one of her most gallant sons. My research commenced in January 2006, and after many amazing twists and turns, delays and dead ends, I am now privileged to present the life and times of Cornelius McNamara. The information contained in this book was gleaned from many different sources in Ireland, Britain and the United States of America. So, allow me to present to you the story of this fascinating man.

Oil painting of Cornelius McNamara in Volunteer uniform c.1917, taken from a black and white print.

List of Abbreviations

ASU	Active Service Unit
Batt.	Battalion
Bde	Brigade
CO	Commanding Officer
Col.	Colonel
Comdt	Commandant (Irish equivalent of a British Army Major)
Comdt-Gen.	Commandant General
Coy.	Company
DI	District Inspector (RIC)
DORA	The Defence of the Realm Act
FS	Free State
GAA	Gaelic Athletic Association
Gen.	General
GHQ	General Headquarters
HSE	Health Services Executive
I/O	Intelligence Officer
IRA	Irish Republican Army
IRB	Irish Republican Brotherhood
IRPDF	Irish Republican Prisoners' Dependents' Fund
Lt	Lieutenant (British)
O/C	Officer Commanding
QM	Quartermaster
RIC	Royal Irish Constabulary
RUC	Royal Ulster Constabulary
Vol.	Volunteer

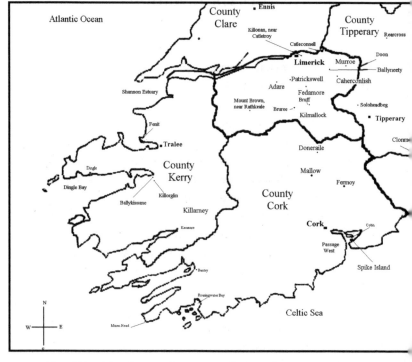

Map of Limerick and surrounding counties. Illustration by James McMahon.

His Early Life

Cornelius McNamara, better known to his friends and fellow Volunteers as Connie Mackey, lived at 1 Blackboy Pike, off Mulgrave Street. He was described to me as a short, stocky man, quiet and humble, with brown hair and brown eyes. He entered this world on 6 April 1896, the only child of Michael McNamara, a pork butcher, and Mary (*née* Greot), of Blackboy Pike, and was named after his grandfather Cornelius McNamara. On 28 April 1900, when Connie was just four years old, his mother Mary died after a four-month battle with TB, in the City Home Hospital, Limerick. Three years later, his father Michael married Hanorah Minihan and they had seven children; Patrick, Tom, Mamie, Babe, Michael, Josie and Christopher.

Like so many of his contemporaries, Cornelius received his formative education in the Christian Brothers School, Sexton Street, Limerick, which, a century on, continues to be one of the leading learning establishments in the region. He started in primary school around the age of five in 1901, and then, when around twelve years old, he attended the secondary school, staying for a few years before leaving around the age of fourteen to become an apprentice butcher. On finishing his apprenticeship he became a butcher in one of the large bacon factories in Limerick, just like his father, probably working in Shaw's on Mulgrave Street, which was just down the road from his house in Blackboy Pike. Cornelius was a keen hurler and a member of the Faughs GAA club, which drew its membership from the region around Ballysimon and Blackboy Pike.

Connie's father and stepmother, Michael and Hanora McNamara.

Pádraig Pearse and Roger Casement came to Limerick in early 1914 to raise Volunteer companies. Connie did not join up straight away like so many others. As the eldest, he chose to remain at home to help his parents and family, although he was very much aware of how the Volunteer numbers in Limerick were increasing. The following year, in October 1915, Connie joined the Volunteer movement, but remained in his trade to finance his activities.

1916: The Easter Rising

In October 1915, aged nineteen, Connie enlisted in 'C' company Limerick City Battalion, under Commandant Michael Colivet.[1] Connie joined the Volunteers because Ireland, and of course Limerick, was under British rule at the time. The principal employers in Limerick were Protestant families, descendants of English settlers. The suffering of the Irish famine (1846-1849) would still have been in living memory for grandparents. The injustices handed out under a foreign occupation ignited a spark and a thirst for freedom. A Gaelic revival was underway, and people were starting to express their Irishness.

The Gaelic League was founded in 1893 in order to promote the Irish language. The Irish language was read and understood by a large percentage of the population; non-speakers and those with limited knowledge were encouraged to attend language classes. Michael Collins also went to Irish language classes, while a resident in London in 1909. The GAA was founded in Thurles on 1 November 1884, with the purpose of promoting the national games, hurling and Gaelic football, but with an emphasis on all aspects of Irish culture. The Volunteer movement, meanwhile, gave men of fighting spirit the avenue to liberate Ireland by the use of physical force. Connie was a keen hurler and the content of his Gormanstown diary shows he could both read and write Irish.[2]

This book is a biography of Connie's life, and it is set against the local and national events of those turbulent times. The Easter Rising, the War of Independence and the Civil War have been extensively documented. I have delved into the historical background to give relevance to Connie's activities and actions while in the Limerick City Battalion, and also 'A' Company, Second Battalion, Mid-Limerick Brigade.

The Irish Volunteers were founded at the Rotunda meeting in Dublin on 25 November 1913. The first company to be formed outside Dublin was Athlone, and the second, in Dromcollogher, Co. Limerick. The early formation of the Dromcollogher Company was due to Fr Tom Wall, the parish curate. A meeting was held in the Athenaeum Hall in Cecil Street, Limerick on Sunday, 25 January 1914, to inaugurate a corps of Volunteers in the city. The Athenaeum then became the Royal Cinema in 1939 and now stands derelict.[3] The meeting was addressed by Pádraig Pearse and Roger Casement and practically every man present enrolled. Offices were opened in No. 1 Hartstonge Street and soon there were sufficient numbers to allow for the formation of eight companies. Connie was eighteen years old and fully aware of these goings-on, the early seeds of joining the Volunteer movement were planted in his mind. Mary Spring Rice, of Mount Trenchard near Foynes, helped to plan and finance the famous Howth gun-running expedition. She was aboard the yacht *Asgard* with her friends Erskine Childers and wife, when guns were landed at Howth, Co. Dublin, on 26 July 1914.[4]

The Limerick City Battalion numbered around 1,250 men. After the onset of the Great War, John Redmond, leader of the Irish Parliamentary Party, voiced his belief that a measure of self-government would eventually be granted to Ireland. He also held the view that such an eventuality would stave off partition in the North.[5] Redmond supported the British war effort; the result was that the Volunteer movement split in September 1914. In Limerick, over 1,000 men sided with Redmond, and became known as the National Volunteers.

A lifelong friend of Connie's, Paddy O'Toole, supported the Redmond faction and enlisted in the Connaught Rangers during the First World War. After the war, he became a quartermaster in the Mid–Limerick Brigade, IRA. However, most of the 150 guns that were acquired before the split remained in the hands of the Volunteers who remained loyal to the original aims of the movement. William Lawlor was the only instructor that had not gone over to the Redmond camp, and it was feared that this would have a disastrous effect on the training programme. However on 24 November 1914, Captain Robert Monteith of 'A' Company of the Dublin Brigade was banished from Dublin by the British authorities due to his Republican activities. He then came straight to Limerick, where he proved himself a valuable asset by assisting Ernest Blythe with the training of the Limerick Volunteers.[6]

Soon after the formation of the Volunteers in Limerick, a branch of Cumann na mBan, the women's auxiliary unit of the Irish Volunteers, was started as well. The first meeting was held in the Gaelic League Rooms as the majority of those attending were members of the Gaelic League. Madge Daly was elected president, a position she held until 1924, except for 1921, when Mrs O'Callaghan, the wife of the murdered Mayor Michael O'Callaghan, took the position. Classes were started immediately in first aid, home nursing, drill, signalling and also instruction in the use of arms. Subscriptions were donated at meetings and functions; all monies raised went to the Volunteers' arms fund. The Redmondite split of September 1914 had little or no effect on the Volunteer ladies in Limerick, however the Redmond faction did start the National Volunteer Ladies Association, which had their head-quarters in O'Connell Street, but they soon faded away.[7]

On 15 February 1915, Padráig Pearse, director of military organisation for the Volunteers, was also on the IRB's supreme council and its secret military council, the core group that began planning for a rising. He wrote to the Limerick City Battalion, 'There are many who think that the Limerick City Battalion is the best we have. There are good men in com-mand of it; men whose loyalty, courage and prudence are not surpassed in Ireland.'

The nucleus of the Volunteers in Limerick City comprised of three men, Commandant of the Limerick Brigade, Michael P. Colivet; Vice-Commandant, honorary Colonel James Leddin, and Adjutant George (Seoirse) Clancy. Three weeks before the Rising, Colivet, Connie's commanding officer, was ordered by GHQ in Dublin to speed up his battalion and brigade organisation as events were now reaching a climax. He had eight battalions under his command but only the Limerick City Battalion, which Connie was attached to, was reasonably well armed. Furthermore, Colivet's battalions were less than full strength, numbering no more than 200 men each, whereas a battalion should have comprised of at least 500 men. Connie's battalion never mustered more than 205. At best, Colivet could count on no more than 1,600 men and these were far outnumbered by the better-armed British forces, whose strength was around 3,000 men in Limerick.[8]

In the autumn of 1915, Pearse outlined the general plan for the Rising for Austin Stack, a member of the IRB and commandant of the Kerry Brigade, and Alfred Cotton, also a member of the IRB and a captain in the Kerry Brigade.

The plan was that the Cork Volunteers would move towards Macroom and link up with the Kerry Brigade, who in turn, would be in communication with Volunteers in Clare, Limerick and Galway. A line would eventually be held from the Shannon, through Limerick and East Kerry, to Macroom. The units of the Irish Volunteers in Ulster would then occupy positions from the Shannon to the south of Ulster. The Rising would begin with the Declaration of the Republic and the seizure of Dublin, with attacks against British troops in adjoining counties. Country Volunteer forces would move towards the capital to relieve the pressure on the Volunteers who had seized a ring of positions inside it.[9]

The arms and ammunition were to be landed at Fenit harbour in Tralee Bay, Co. Kerry, from the German arms ship *Aud*, and distributed to the Kerry, Cork, Galway and Limerick Volunteers. Stack and Cotton were to have a goods train ready to leave Fenit with the arms. Part of the armament was to be left at Tralee, for distribution to the Cork and Kerry Brigades and the remainder sent by goods train to Limerick, where arrangements would be made to dispatch them to the Galway area. At Fenit, a pilot would have to be on the alert for signals agreed upon with the arms ship, in order to meet it and guide it into the pier. A cable code was to be sent to the USA announcing the proclamation of the Republic. Everything, as far as the south and west were concerned, depended on the safe arrival of the *Aud* and the distribution of the arms to the waiting Volunteers.[10]

The Volunteer leaders originally asked that the *Aud* be in Tralee Bay between 20 and 23 April. After all the arrangements were in place, GHQ then made their fatal error. They decided that, 'Arms must not be landed before night of Sunday, 23.' They believed if the arms were landed earlier, the British would be alerted and strike at them before the arms were received.[11] By the time this message reached Germany via America, the *Aud* was already on her way to Ireland, and she did not have wireless equipment. The plans for a nationwide insurrection were now doomed. The Volunteer leaders in Dublin knew nothing of this and would only learn of it when it was too late. They went ahead with their preparations for the Rising.[12]

Limerick was a key area in the insurrection plans. On Tuesday 18 April, Capt. Sean Fitzgibbon arrived in Limerick from Dublin headquarters with instructions for Colivet from Pearse. These new instructions clashed with the plan of operations, which the Limerick Brigade had worked out. According to Colivet's new instructions, he was to receive the arms from Fenit in nearby Abbeyfeale, then take his requirements for his own area, and take the rest of the arms to Galway. Police and military positions in Limerick City were to be attacked to cover the transfer of the arms train safely across the Clare line at Limerick station. These new instructions were so different from his original instructions that Colivet decided to go to Dublin to have the matter clarified by Pearse himself.[13]

The next day, he met Pearse at the North Star Hotel, near Dublin's Amiens Street Station. Pearse confirmed his instructions and told Colivet to cancel all previous plans and concentrate on the arms landing. Colivet asked Pearse point blank, 'This means insurrection as soon as the arms are landed and we get them?' Pearse replied, 'Yes and you are to start at 7.00p.m. on Sunday. You are to proclaim the Republic and as soon as things are secure in your own district, move eastwards.' Finally, Colivet was then told he would have to work out the local details himself. So, at less than a week's notice, Colivet had to plan in detail the part Limerick was to play in the Easter Rising.[14]

As soon as Colivet arrived back in Limerick, he summoned his brigade staff to a meeting at the home of George (Seoirse) Clancy, in the North Strand. It was renamed Clancy's Strand in his honour after his brutal murder on 6 March 1921. Finally it was agreed that Connie's Limerick City Battalion should march out of the city at 10.00a.m. Sunday, to Killonan, Co. Limerick, as if for the previously announced three-day manoeuvres. The return to the city was timed for 7.00p.m., when all police and military barracks in the city were to be attacked, after telegraphic and telephone wires had first been cut, as well as railway communications with Limerick Junction and Dublin. It was intended that the police and military garrisons were to be confined to their barracks by the attack, acting as a diversion until the Kerry arms train had passed safely into Clare. When the arms reached Limerick, the barrack attacks were to be followed through until the buildings were taken.[15]

As the train had to cross the Limerick lines to the south unnoticed and uninterrupted, the police and military diversion was essential. At Newcastle West on the following day, the Volunteers were to be posted to take over the train at Abbeyfeale, and to attack the police barracks in Newcastle West and see the train through safely. They were also to attack and disarm any police likely to interfere with the plans. The Volunteer unit at Newcastle West was to watch the station very closely, as it was a terminus where all trains had to be reversed, and the delay offered opportunities for police and military interference. GHQ issued an order that any armed clash with police and military must be avoided until 7.00p.m. on Sunday. The Limerick plan provided for all available Volunteers to be armed and taken aboard the train as it proceeded towards Limerick. In Co. Clare,

Captain Michael Brennan and the Mid-Clare and East Clare Volunteers were to seize Ennis and all stations to Crusheen, and finally, after disarming the RIC in various localities, take up positions north of the Shannon at Limerick, complete its encirclement, and force a surrender of hostile forces within.

In summary, the Cork, Clare, Tipperary and West Limerick Volunteers were to seize railways and barracks in their immediate areas, disarm the police, surround Limerick and march to relieve Connie and the City Battalion. The plan assumed that the barracks would be taken without a hitch, that the police would be overcome, that the arms train would pass without interference, and most of all, the arms would be safely landed from the *Aud*.[16]

On Good Friday morning, wireless experts left Dublin for Killarney. They were: Denis Daly, Con Keating, Donal Sheehan, Charles Monaghan and Colm O'Lochlainn. They were to dismantle the Cahirciveen station and set up the transmitter in Tralee. It was a fruitless journey, as the ship would be gone before they reached Kerry and in fact it did not actually carry any radio equipment. Waiting for the Volunteers at Killarney were two cars from Limerick City; one driven by its owner, Tommy McInerney, (who was later imprisoned with Connie in Cork Male Gaol and Spike Island), and the other by Sam Windrim. Denis Daly and Colm O'Lochlainn got into Sam Windrim's car and the three others went with Tommy McInerney. John Quilty, who was unable to travel because of a domestic problem, owned the second car. In darkness the two cars became separated and just beyond Killorglin, Co. Kerry, McInerney took a wrong turn and the car plunged off Ballykissane pier into the sea. He was rescued by a local man and later arrested. Tragically, his three fellow travellers were drowned; thus Con Keating, Donal Sheehan and Charles Monaghan became the first casualties of the Easter Rising. Worse still, the Volunteers never erected the two green signal lights at the designated landing place, which caused both the arms ship and the submarine to sail up and down Tralee Bay waiting in vain for a signal that would never come.[17]

The previous day, Holy Thursday, Captain Karl Spindler, in command of the *Aud*, arrived in Tralee Bay, according to his original instructions, and found there was no one to meet him on his arrival. He sailed into Tralee Bay, flashed his signals and waited in vain for the green signals that would prompt the unloading of the arms. The next day, after he had been twenty-four hours in Tralee Bay, and after having had to bluff his way out of an encounter with the captain of a British vessel, he began to steam away from Fenit and towards the open sea. Soon, the *Lord Heneage*, an armed trawler, and two other British warships were sent to intercept him and bring him to Queenstown port. He was intercepted and escorted back to Queenstown port, but before he got there he ordered his men to change into German Naval uniforms and he transferred them into small boats, leaving timed explosives behind on the *Aud*. The enormous blast not only destroyed his ship, but also destroyed the Volunteers arms and any chance of the Rising succeeding.[18]

Earlier on Good Friday, the captain of the German submarine U-19, Lieutenant Wiesbach, had also waited in vain for the prearranged signal. Even though he had seen Spindler, he had made no effort to contact him, concentrating instead on looking for the green lights that were never to signal him. He eventually made a decision; rather than put his submarine at risk by waiting around, he put Roger Casement and his companions ashore in an inflatable boat at around 2.30a.m., and sped off to open sea. Casement was arrested shortly after midday, and a few hours later Austin Stack, Commandant of the Kerry Brigade, who had been helping make preparations for the landing of arms, was arrested also.[19]

As the tragic news from Kerry trickled through, the local Volunteer commands were in a confused state. In Limerick City, Colivet dispatched Lieutenant Whelan to Tralee to find out the position there. When no word came from Dublin, Colivet sent out dispatches cancelling all arrangements in his command for the time being but with the warning that further orders were to follow. He sent Lieutenant Seamus Gubbins to Dublin by afternoon train. Gubbins met Seán Mac Diarmada and was told that the Rising would defiantly take place. Gubbins sent the prearranged coded telegram to Limerick, 'The books have arrived'. The Rising was on.[20]

On Holy Saturday, Colivet was so concerned that he sent Captain Liam Forde off to the same destination on a similar mission. (Forde would later become Connie's Commanding Officer, when the latter was made commandant of the Mid-Limerick Brigade, in March 1921.) Forde also went to Mac Diarmada's lodgings, and confided to him the latest news from Kerry and Limerick, as well as a suggestion from Colivet that, in view of what had happened, the Rising should be postponed. Mac Diarmada insisted the Rising must take place, even if they only had sticks and stones to fight with. On Easter Sunday, the *Sunday Independent* published an order from the IRA chief of staff, Eoin Mac Neill, calling off the Easter 'manoeuvres'. This threw the country Volunteers into utter confusion. On hearing Mac Neill's countermanding order, Mac Diarmada was inconsolable. He walked to Liberty Hall with Forde. He said 'they should rise, if only with pikes and bayonets, even though defeated, their blood would regenerate the nation'.[21]

When Forde arrived at Liberty Hall, he had breakfast with Clarke, Connelly and Ceannt and they were waited on by Countess Markievicz. The other three left after breakfast to attend a meeting which lasted until about 4.00p.m. Pearse emerged and told him that everything was off for the present but to hold themselves in readiness for further orders. Pearce provided a motor car for Forde to travel to Cashel to convey a message to Pierce McCann, Commandant of the Tipperary Volunteers. After he conveyed this message, Forde hired another car at Cashel and reported back to the Limerick Volunteer Command at midnight.[22]

On Easter Saturday and Easter Sunday, Connie, with 'C' Company Limerick City Battalion, responded to general

The Limerick City Battalion at Killonan, Easter Sunday 1916. (*Image kindly supplied by Limerick Museum.*)

orders from Colivet for swift mobilisation of the battalion. He was at Killonan for the Easter Rising. Each man was ordered to bring two days' rations and to get confession, and each was provided with a first aid kit. About 125 men, 82 per cent of the battalion, paraded for action. On Easter Sunday morning, O'Rahilly arrived in Limerick with written instructions for Colivet from Mac Neill stating, 'Volunteers completely deceived. All orders for tomorrow, Sunday, cancelled.' Colivet immediately issued final orders cancelling arrangements for outside units of his command, but decided to take the Limerick City Battalion to Killonan and camp out there as if nothing had happened. When word came that the Rising was called off, Connie and the Limerick City Battalion marched back to Limerick. They were facing over 3,000 British troops; each man in the brigade was given an extra 100 rounds of ammunition, as they expected to be attacked by the British on their return from Killonan.[23]

On Easter Sunday, a proclamation was posted outside every barracks in Limerick City to the effect that any man caught with arms or ammunition was guilty of high treason, and liable to be shot. The men of the Limerick City Battalion spent the next three or four nights removing ammunition from the battalion headquarters to places of safety. Immediately after Easter Week, all the officers of the Limerick City Battalion were arrested. Later they claimed that they were the first in Ireland to organise after Easter week and the first to parade in public after the Rising.[24]

Towards the end of Easter week, Sir Anthony Weldon, the British Commander in Limerick, sent a demand for the surrender of their arms through the Mayor of Limerick, James Quinn. A meeting of the combined board of officers decided to refuse this demand, which was several times repeated through the Mayor and rejected every time. Sir Anthony then decided on a show of force; he paraded three infantry regiments, a cavalry regiment and an artillery brigade of eighteen guns through the city. When the Volunteers were faced with seizure of their arms, they decided to hand over their arms to the Mayor, in order to avoid bloodshed. There was a proviso that each Volunteer should hand over his arms to Colivet, who would then surrender them to the Mayor. The arms were handed over in the council chamber of the town hall, on Friday 5 May 1916, in the presence of Wealdon and other British officers. The Volunteers had in fact rendered most of them useless, by removing the rifle bolts, or pouring acid down the barrels. Some of the rifles were so completely destroyed they were surrendered in haversacks. Liam Forde and six other Volunteers kept hold of their rifles as they did not agree with the handover and intended to use them in the future.[25]

The Limerick City Battalion at Killonan, Easter Sunday, 1916. (*Image kindly supplied by Limerick Museum.*)

1917: The Second Battalion and the IRB

The handover of their arms, together with their failure to go to the aid of the Volunteers in Dublin during the Easter Rising, caused a lot of enmity within the Limerick City Battalion. In March 1917, Ernest Blythe, Peadar McMahon and Peadar Dunne arrived in Limerick from Dublin on a recruitment campaign to form the Second Battalion. Most of the men of fighting spirit, who were unhappy with the events of the Easter Rising, left the First Battalion and joined this new battalion, including officers Liam Forde, and Michael Hartney.[26]

The local GAA in Limerick was instrumental in setting up the Second Battalion. The members of a number of junior hurling clubs promptly enlisted, and five companies in each of the different districts in Limerick City were duly formed. The junior hurling clubs became identified with a local Sinn Féin club and they in turn sponsored a new Company of Volunteers in that area. Faughs hurling club in the Ballysimon–Blackboy Pike area sponsored the P.H. Pearse Sinn Féin club, which became 'A' Company. Connie was one of the first to join 'A' Company when it was formed. St Patrick's and Claughan clubs, from the Pennywell and Park districts, sponsored the Thomas Ashe Sinn Féin club which, in turn, sponsored 'B' Company. Likewise, the Star hurling club from the Irishtown district was affiliated with the Roger Casement Sinn Féin club, and resulted in the forming of 'C' Company. Shamrock, on the Boherbuoy side of the city, sponsored the Con Colbert Sinn Féin club, which, in turn, became 'D' Company. Treaty hurl-

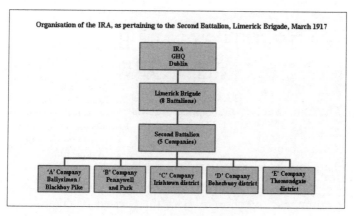

Organisation plan of the Second Battalion, March 1917.

ing club on the Thomondgate side of the city, was identified with the Ned Daly Sinn Féin club, which then formed 'E' Company.[27] These five companies then merged to form the Second Battalion. Peadar Dunne was appointed O/C, Peadar McMahon was appointed Vice-O/C, Robert Byrne was appointed adjutant, and Martin Barry was made quartermaster. The First Limerick City Battalion continued with Michael Colivet as O/C and George (Seoirse) Clancy as adjutant.

After the Second Battalion was formed, there was a great deal of animosity between the two battalions, which lasted right up to the end of the Civil War. Many members of the original battalion felt that the new battalion was usurping their position, while those in the new battalion resented the inaction of the officers during 1916 and the fact that the leaders of the Limerick City Battalion handed their weapons over to the British without firing a single shot. Hopkinson, in his book *The War of Independence,* also states there were class barriers between the two battalions. The First Battalion was

Orders for a Funeral Firing Party
(Taken from an Irish Army Manual for use with the Rifle "Lee Enfield 303 Mk 2")

The Firing Party consisted of an Officer/Sergeant, and six men. The senior officer gives the orders and the six men carry out the drill and fire over the graveside. There may have been a bugler as well, sounding the last post.

1. When the Firing Party are at the graveside they are there before everyone else and are at a position of Reversed Arms.
2. When the Funeral cortege arrives they are brought to "Attention while resting on Arms Reversed". The Irish order is "A Mheitheal - Aire"
3. They then "Present Arms from the resting on Arms Reversed". The Irish order is "Tairgg Airm"
4. From there they are told to "load the Blank Cartridges". The Irish Order is "Carcai (Le Cartus Bhalbha)- Lodail.
5. From there the Firing Party are told "Tairgg" which they then put the index finger on the trigger ready to fire, and the final order is "Lamhach" where they fire the blank round.

So, this order is repeated a total of three times
a. Lodail
b. Tairgg
c. Lamhach

The Bugler (if present) then blows the last post after the volley of shots is fired and the firing party are at the position of the salute with their rifles.

The funeral drill is then finished for the firing party and the Irish Flag is then removed from the coffin as it is lowered into the grave.

Orders for a Funeral Firing Party. These would have been the commands that Connie would have given to his firing parties for the Volunteer funerals.

associated with white-collar workers, whereas the Second was associated more with the working class.

Limerick's Fighting Story, published by Kerryman Press in 1949, stated that 'A' Company was based in Thomond and 'E' Company in Blackboy Pike. But according to Connie's IRA Pension Statement, 'A' Company was based around Blackboy Pike. This is also supported by various IRA Second Battalion lists. In early 1917, Connie became a member of the P.H. Pearse Sinn Féin club, and he remained a member of Sinn Féin until he joined Fianna Fáil in its formation in 1926. 'A' company was based at Blackboy Pike, a mile from Limerick City centre and close to Mount St Lawrence cemetery. Connie assisted in organising firing parties at Volunteer funerals, and also the safe transport of arms to the firing parties.[28] The orders were in Irish and the procedure remains virtually unchanged to the present day.

Connie was in command of most firing parties in Mount St Lawrence cemetery with the exception of the firing party for the funeral of Adjutant Robert Byrne, for reasons that I have dealt with in the chapter dedicated to his rescue.

The first priority for the Limerick City Battalions was to replace the weapons handed over to the British in 1916, and so Connie helped QM Martin Barry in rearming the Second Battalion. Connie raided for arms and ammunition wherever possible, usually from sources such as prominent Loyalist families, retired British Army officers, captured Crown personnel and small RIC barracks. Early in 1917, in one such raid, Connie and 'A' company raided the home of a Mr Corby, in Rosbrien, Co. Limerick, but the quantity of arms they came away with was not recorded. The majority of operations were intelligence led, based on information provided by the company or battalion I/O. Among other things in his battalion area, he would have an accurate list of all cars, with their registration numbers, names of owners and a general description of how friendly they were. There was also a list of homes available to men on the run, a list of homes of people who possessed arms and the types of arms therein, and a list of local stores that stocked arms and ammunition, e.g. Nestor's Sport Shop in O'Connell Street. (This became a licensed premises in 1998.)

Connie was appointed dispatch rider to Battalion Commandant, Captain Peadar Dunne, later brigade O/C, and Vice-Commandant Peadar McMahon. His home in Blackboy Pike, just off Mulgrave Street, was a humble two-bedroom abode with no electricity or running water; fresh water was obtained from an outside pump and there was an outside toilet in the back garden. On the other side of Mulgrave Street, about 200 yards away, was situated the Blackboy Pike RIC Barracks, which was one of the smaller RIC barracks. Also, less than half a mile down Mulgrave Street, was the Ordnance Barracks used by the British military. Connie's home became a dispatch centre from 1917, until his arrest in 1920. It was also used as a storehouse for weapons; the chimney had a hollowed-out secret compartment where small arms such as grenades, pistols and ammunition could be stored. Curiously, the chimney is the only part of the house that still survives. Connie would not have been able to use his home for these activities without the full support of his parents, and also the assistance of his brothers and sisters. It was a family affair, and all members of the McNamara household took part in helping the Volunteers in one way or another. Later, when they came of age, Patrick and Thomas followed in their brother's foot-steps and became Volunteers in 'A' Company. Had the War of Independence continued, there is no doubt that the rest of his brothers and sisters would have become Volunteers too.

Connie was responsible for sending and receiving dispatches and communications from all over the county, and monitoring the movements of both the IRA and British forces. During this period, he delivered all kinds of communication almost daily; verbal and written, covering an extensive area, includ-ing Castleconnell, Killonan, Patrickswell, Adare, Kildimo and Ballyneety. He delivered dispatches to the East and West Limerick Brigades, as well as to his own and to the neighbour-ing brigades in surrounding counties. Though Crown Forces frequently detained him, he always succeeded in getting his dis-patches through.[29] Unsurprisingly, given the amount of activity he was involved in, he became familiar to the British military. This resulted in his home being subjected to frequent raids by Crown Forces, with the intention of procuring intelligence, weapons and flushing out prisoners. His home backed onto Mount St Lawrence cemetery and as soon as a patrol was seen coming towards the house, the Volunteers inside it jumped over the back wall and escaped through the graveyard. Although his home was small in size the effect it had was enormous and indeed quite a few men of 'A' Company came from the humble houses of Blackboy Pike. All the activities of the house were carried out under the very noses of the nearby RIC and Ordnance Barracks. The McNamara family frequently had to sleep on the floor underneath the windows, as the Black and Tans would occasionally drive by at night and machine-gun the house. In a significant development and in recognition of his services, Peadar McMahon presented Connie with a rifle. Due to the scarcity of weapons at this time, this was deemed

Above left: An early picture of Connie in Volunteer uniform, c.1917. It is not known which side the dog was on, or why he was being held prisoner by Connie.

Above right: Connie in a Volunteer uniform c.1917, probably at the same unknown location.

an honour. Rifles would only have been given to the most reliable of men.

Later in 1917, Connie had the privilege of being admitted into the fourth division of the IRB, an honour offered to only the most dedicated of the Volunteers. The IRB, wanting to ensure there would be no surrender the next time the Volunteers went into combat, put its chosen personnel in key positions within the movement. Connie was probably chosen on two fronts, his home had been used as a dispatch centre, which key IRB men in Limerick would have frequented, and he was recognised as a potential leader of men. He was sworn in by Commandant John Sweeny, and witnessed by Organiser (a rank within the IRB) Martin Barry. The president of the IRB at that time was Thomas Ashe.[30] The oath taken would have read:

> In the presence of God, I, Cornelius McNamara, do solemnly swear that I will do my utmost to establish the independence of Ireland, and that I will bear true allegiance to the Supreme Council of the Irish Republican Brotherhood and the Government of the Irish Republic and implicitly obey the constitution of the Irish Republican Brotherhood and all my superior officers and that I will preserve inviolably the secrets of the organisation.

The Irish Republican Brotherhood (IRB), was a small, secret, revolutionary body (known as the Fenian movement in the 1850s and 60s), committed to the use of force to establish an independent Irish Republic. It was led by an eleven-member Supreme Council, consisting of representatives from the seven districts in which the organisation was active: the Irish provinces of Ulster, Munster, Leinster, and Connacht, as well as Scotland

and the north and south of England. Four other members were co-opted, and together this council elected three of its members to the executive roles of president, secretary, and treasurer.[31]

Its president from the summer of 1919 was Michael Collins, who was also a chief organising force behind the IRA. With Collins as leader, the IRB accepted the Anglo-Irish Treaty agreed by him and the British Government in 1921 as compatible with its aims. It dissolved itself in 1924.

Connie attended all the Second Battalion parades; at that time all foot drills and commands were given in Irish, just as they are in the present Irish Army. As he progressed within the Volunteer movement, Connie was given more and more responsibilities. He started to give regular musketry instruction, conduct rifle practice and give training in the use of hand grenades.[32] Connie also trained his men in drill practice for parades and route marches in the local countryside. Volunteers generally surrendered their spare time to drill on evenings and weekends. Connie had to balance such responsibilities with his IRB duties.

The IRB Constitution, as published by the Supreme Council, stated that a unit of the IRB was known as a circle, which elected a centre and a sub-centre, and that each circle was subdivided into sections of not more than ten men. Each section was in the command of a section leader. He was required to have a deep insight into each man under his command, and to hand subscriptions to the treasurer, as well as having to submit a report on any man absent from the montly circle meetings. A monthly subscription of sixpence was the norm, while contributions to war materials, according to means, were also expected.[33]

1918: Promotion and the Conscription Crisis

From the day of his introduction to the Volunteers, Connie's every move was watched by friend and foe alike. From the earliest days he was viewed as a man of tremendous ability and leadership potential, and in February 1918, he was appointed Second Lieutenant of 'A' Company, the start of his rise through the ranks. During the year, he underwent specialist training, attending Morse code and special signalling classes. He also assisted Battalion QM Martin Barry, in procuring arms and ammunition from enemy forces through various raids and by holding up patrols. On one occasion Connie managed to capture engineering equipment from Crown Forces.[34]

Connie's stepbrothers Patrick and Thomas had also been educated at CBS, Sexton Street, and like their older brother they had left secondary school to become apprentice butchers. Connie's home had been a dispatch centre for a year at this stage, and there were always Volunteers present; officers like Martin Barry, Peadar Dunn, Robert Byrne and Peadar McMahon, who would have discussed, in great detail, the goings-on in Limerick and the rest of the country. This had a big influence on Connie's stepbrothers, and they would have been privy to almost everything that was happening in the Second Battalion. In February, following Connie's example, Patrick joined 'A' Company at the tender age of fourteen, under Captain William Keane. Thomas, aged thirteen, joined Na Fianna Éireann, which was the Volunteer youth movement. Patrick started his service as a scout, delivering messages to the East and West Brigades and transporting revolvers and small arms from one place to

Connie and Patrick at an unknown location.
Connie is on the far left and Patrick is on
the far right.

another from the company arms dumps. As he got older, he took a more active part in the activities that the Active Service Unit of 'A' Company was involved in. He continued to support himself during his service with the family trade.[35]

Not much has been documented about the activities of Connie's stepbrother Thomas, but like Connie and Patrick he did become an apprentice butcher at around fourteen years of age, after leaving secondary school. He became a Volunteer shortly after, delivering messages and acting as a scout. When he was delivering messages, he would wear two pairs of socks and put the message between them. If his house was being watched, he would sneak out the back window and escape through Mount St Lawrence cemetery. If the message had to be delivered some distance away, there would be a bicycle waiting for him at a prearranged place in the cemetery. His mother Hanora would always stay up, waiting for him to return from delivering his dispatches. Like Patrick, he also transported weapons from one place to another, and as he got older he too became more active in 'A' Company's activities.[36]

During the early part of 1918, the British Army was running short on troops for the Western Front. To address this, on 18 April, a Bill for conscription in Ireland (the Military Service Bill) was voted through at Westminster. Even though there were large numbers of Irishmen (and especially Limerick men) in the British Army, the idea of forced conscription in Ireland created a backlash. All the country's political parties and the Catholic hierarchy were unified in opposition to the Bill. On 20 April 1918, the Anti-Conscription Committee was formed in Dublin to devise plans to resist conscription in Ireland. The same day, Catholic Bishops of Ireland held their annual conference at Maynooth. As a result of both assemblies came a pledge to be taken at the church door of every parish in Ireland, 'Denying the right of the British Government to enforce compulsory service in this country, we pledge ourselves solemnly to one another to resist conscription by the most effective means at our disposal.' Soon there were Anti-Conscription rallies nationwide. On 21 April, nearly one million people signed the pledge in Dublin. Huge numbers of people all over Ireland joined the Volunteers as a result. On 23 April, there was a one-day national strike; the whole country almost closed down, and even the pubs were shut.

The Volunteers were fully aware of the situation, which could bring them back into armed conflict with the British. In Limerick, as the numbers of Volunteers started to swell, the Anti-Conscription campaign started to build momentum. Patrick was chosen, as well as other men from the Second Battalion, to prevent young men in Limerick City from joining the British Army, a task carried out by either coercion or intimidation. Connie and Patrick helped Martin Barry in the distribution of pikes and other emergency supplies throughout the area, including food and medical supplies, which would have gone to feed men on the run in safe houses and men made destitute by the British. Although pikes had long been made obsolete as weapons of war, their use as a recruiting symbol to the Volunteers in Limerick, cannot be underestimated. They would have been used to remind people of the siege of Limerick of 1691, when the people of Limerick also resisted the British Army. The crest of the Limerick City Battalion was the Treaty Stone crossed with two pikes.[37]

These campaigns ensured conscription was never introduced in Ireland, even though 200,000 to 300,000 Irishmen enlisted with British forces during the Great War.[38] The conscription

The cap badge of the Limerick City Battalion. (*Image kindly supplied by Limerick Museum.*)

A page from the Gormanstown autograph book, showing the Limerick City Battalion crest.

crisis produced a considerable rise in Volunteer membership and it was this event that unified the Church and moderate opinion with the Sinn Féin outlook. Over 2,000 new members enlisted in Limerick, but when the threat of conscription faded, many of the newer Volunteers left as quickly as they had joined. However, the event propelled Sinn Féin to the position of the dominant political party in Ireland.

But as the Volunteer movement began to build momentum, the gaols started to fill up again. Cumann na mBan, working closely with Irish Republican Prisoners' Dependents' Fund (IRPDF), were busily engaged attending to the needs of prisoners and their families, visiting them, arranging for meals, etc. On occasion, men were arrested in the neighbouring counties of Kerry and Tipperary and brought to Limerick Prison. Little information was forwarded to their families by the authorities, but the ladies intervened and contacted the families with updates.[39]

The Volunteer movement recognised early on that it was usually the breadwinner of the family that was being imprisoned, and that their families needed to have financial support to save them from poverty or starvation. The IRPDF was set up in 1917, and its first president was the Limerick man Éamon de Valera. The main purpose of the fund was to raise monies and distribute aid to the families of imprisoned Volunteers. Later on, during the War of Independence, it looked after the families of deceased Republicans, and also helped with funeral costs. The fund was tolerated by the British; it was allowed to be advertised in the daily papers in Ireland, and it was also promoted in the Irish communities in Britain and America. Public collections were organised, with additional funds collected during meetings of Cumann na mBan and

Fianna Éireann. Needy families applied for a grant from the fund, which was then paid to them weekly.

Patrick assisted QM Thomas Lawlor in making an ammunition dump in the latter's back field in Ballysimon, which then became one of the Company's ammunition dumps. Patrick was also in charge of bringing arms from the dump for different operations; afterwards he was entrusted with the responsibility of returning them to the dump and cleaning the rifles for future raids and operations.

As a result of the rise in numbers, Volunteer units were growing throughout Co. Limerick, and three new battalions were raised: Castleconnell and Murroe (Third Battalion); Caherconlish and Fedamore (Fourth Battalion); and last but not least, Patrickswell and Adare (Fifth Battalion). A brigade was then organised; the first Brigadier of this new Mid-Limerick Brigade was Peader Dunne, with Michael Colivet as Vice-Commandant. The activities of the First Battalion began

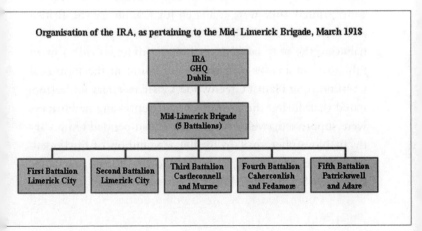

Organisation plan of the Mid-Limerick Brigade, March 1918.

to diminish and after a while, it ceased to be recognised by GHQ. Both battalions were merged in March 1921.[40]

The Mid-Limerick Brigade had their headquarters in the Transport Union Hall, O'Connell Street, in a back attic on top of the four-storey building, which is now the headquarters of the HSE's Child Care and Family Support Services. It was occupied by a small number of staff officers, engaged in sending and receiving dispatches and communications from all over the country. It monitored the movements of both IRA and British forces. Although the military and the police frequently raided the building, they never discovered any incriminating documents.[41]

When a printing press was procured from QM Martin Barry, Connie arranged to have weekly copies of *The Irish Republic* newspaper forwarded to the country areas of Limerick.[42] This was a small, local, Republican newspaper, which promoted the struggle. There were in fact numerous newspapers produced by Republican organisations. When such newspapers were printed, they were tolerated for a while by the British and then suppressed. The Volunteers then responded by distributing the very same paper under a different title. On 19 July 1920, in answer to a written question in the House of Commons, Sir Hamar Greenwood, Chief Secretary for Ireland, stated that during the previous year, twenty-one newspapers were suppressed, twelve of which were suspended temporarily. In November 1918, in further recognition of his leadership abilities, Connie was promoted to First Lieutenant of 'A' Company Second Battalion.[43]

1919: The War of Independence and Robert Byrne

On 21 January 1919, at Soloheadbeg, near Tipperary town, Seán Treacy, Dan Breen, Seán Hogan, Seamus Robinson, Tadhg Crowe, Mick McCormack, Paddy O'Dwyer, Michael Ryan and Seán O'Meara of the South Tipperary Brigade, held up two Royal Irish constables, Patrick McDonnell and James O'Connell, who were transporting gelignite from Tipperary town to a quarry in Soloheadbeg. The constables were immediately killed for not surrendering their explosives; the gelignite was seized and used in several barrack attacks in later months.[44] These were the first shots of the War of Independence, and also the first British casualties.

Connie was a member of 'A' Company's Active Service Unit; a group of hand-picked men specially chosen to be available at a moments notice to do high-risk activities in urban areas, the urban equivalent of the Flying Columns. Both worked very closely with the battalions and brigades that they came in contact with outside their area. The local Volunteers acted as guards, lookouts and scouts for the Active Service Units, and they were provided with food and shelter by the local population.[45]

The Active Service Units were much smaller in number than the Flying Columns, as they were working in an urban environment, and they averaged ten men per unit. However, when attacking large targets like an RIC barracks or lorry convoys, they co-ordinated their attacks with other Volunteers from neighbouring battalions and brigades. They rarely attacked British Army barracks as they were far too large and had far too many men defending them. The only instance of a British Army barracks being overrun in was on 28 September 1920, when Liam Lynch and Ernie O'Malley led the Second Co. Cork Brigade to capture the Mallow Barracks.[46]

Connie usually commanded his unit in the felling of trees, cutting of wires and the blocking of roads; activities to delay or distract the military, but mainly to prevent reinforcements from reaching the RIC barracks under attack. The main attacking force would surround the barracks and the roads would be blocked to prevent reinforcements from reaching the barracks, and providing the opportunity for a hasty escape should the need arise.[47] After the organisation of the Second Battalion, Robert Byrne was elected adjutant and then became Connie's superior officer. On 13 January 1919, Byrne was arrested by the RIC and charged with possession of a revolver and ammunition. He was court-martialled and sentenced to twelve months imprisonment with hard labour. The *Limerick Chronicle* of Tuesday 21, reported:

> Byrne was tried today at a court martial under the Defence of the Realm act (DORA) at the New Barracks.[48] When asked to plead he stated, 'The tribunal represented an army of occupation in Ireland, and being so, the members of the court could not, in his view, be impartial judges.'

Sentence was deferred and later he was given twelve months imprisonment.[49]

Byrne quickly became the Republican prisoners' commandant in Limerick Prison, but he did not want to serve his time in prison as a criminal. He organised a policy of disobedience to gain political status for the Republican prisoners. The prison authorities reacted brutally; the leaders were handcuffed day and night in their cells; they were put on bread and water and solitary confinement. The prisoners led by Byrne then rioted and wrecked their cells. They were, in turn, overpowered by the RIC, and their treatment got worse. They were stripped naked, beaten and left bloodied and bruised in their wrecked cells. Byrne decided to go on hunger strike until political status was given to the prisoners. Robert Byrne started his hunger strike around the third week of February, 1919. After three weeks, he was in bad shape, and the prison authorities became concerned about his condition. Between 6 and 8 March, Byrne was confined to bed in the prison hospital. On 12 March, he was removed to the no.1 ward of Limerick workhouse, or the Union Infirmary, as it was also called.[50] This ward was on the second floor, near the Infirmary gates. While he was there he was guarded by six armed men, day and night.[51]

Commandant Peadar Dunne called a battalion council meeting in Hogan's, next door to Matt Boland's shop in Gerald Griffin Street. Around the table were Captain Michael Hartney, Captain Tommy McInerney, and other officers (probably including Connie). A plan was agreed, ready to be executed on Passion Sunday, 6 April. Twenty-four IRA men were to enter the ward under the guise of visitors, and a covering party of fifteen would be on duty in the corridors and grounds. Connie was among them and although it is unclear which party he was in or his exact role, as a First Lieutenant of the battalion, and also as a member of 'A' Company Active Service Unit, he would have played a key part in the operation. Patrick was ordered by Captain Michael McCann to act as a scout during the rescue.[52]

Present-day St Camillus' Hospital, where Robert Byrne was rescued. It currently accommodates the Limerick City Registrar's office.

The RIC had general orders to shoot prisoners in circumstances where a rescue was attempted. That Sunday afternoon, Robert Byrne was being closely guarded by Sergeant J.F. Goulden, a native of Co. Sligo; Constable J. Tierney of Kilteely; Constable J. Fitzpatrick of Clarina; Constable Martin O'Brien, who was attached to Caherconlish station; Constable T. Spillane of Askeaton station, and Warder John Mahoney, who was on the staff of Limerick Prison.[53]

Michael 'Batty' Stack, Section Leader of 'E' Company, Second Battalion, led the rescue attempt. At three o'clock, Stack checked his watch and blew his whistle in a prearranged signal. The plan was to overpower the guards and rescue Byrne, but as soon as the whistle was blown, Warder Mahoney, Constable Spillane and another policeman ran to the bed and grabbed Byrne as he tried to rise. Constable Spillane had his revolver out, and as Byrne tried to heave himself out of bed, the policeman hurled himself on top of him. Stack then shot Spillane who was trying to choke Byrne. Sometime during the struggle Byrne had been shot and he was bleeding profusely. Stack then shot Constable O'Brien and he fell to the floor, fatally wounded. When O'Brien fell, he landed on the feet of Patrick McNamara, a cousin of Connie's. As Patrick stepped back, the whole of his trouser leg and shoes were covered in the constable's blood.[54]

Clad only in his nightshirt and an overcoat, Byrne staggered down the stairs, supported by two Volunteers. They made their way to the front of the hospital, where a horse-drawn hearse should have been waiting. However, the driver, Dominic Kennedy, had gone round to the mortuary at the back of the hospital by mistake. (Captain Tommy McInerney, of 'C' Company was meant to be driving the hearse, but instead got called away at short notice to take Dan Breen and Seán Hogan to West Limerick.) Between them, they carried Byrne about 300 yards to Hassetts Cross, and that was when they discovered that Byrne has been severely wounded. They stopped a passing pony and trap driven by John Ryan of Knockalisheen near Meelick, Co. Clare, and his daughter Nancy. They brought the wounded IRA man to their labourer's cottage. There, at half past eight on Sunday, 6 April, Robert Byrne died.[55]

As a result, on Wednesday 9 April, Limerick City was made a special military area; barricades manned with military and RIC personnel were erected. Tanks and armoured cars were to be stationed at main roads and bridges. No one was permitted to enter the city without a permit, which was granted by the military. Those who asked for permits had to present themselves to an RIC barracks, where they were vetted. If they were considered a loyal subject they were recommended to the military, who then recorded their details on a card, which was stamped and dated. Several premises were acquired for military purposes, including Shannon rowing club, which was located strategically on Sarsfield Bridge.

The Limerick Trades and Labour Council, as a protest against the Special Military Area, founded the Limerick Soviet on 15 April. A general strike was called and British troops were boycotted. A special strike committee was set up to print their own money and control food prices. The president was John Cronin, and treasurers James Casey and James Carr. Practically the whole city went on strike; more than 14,000 workers were involved. Connie, Patrick, and other members of the Second Battalion were chosen by Michael Brennan to disrupt the permit system by a series of civil disobediences. So, on the evening of Easter Sunday, 20 April 1919, three years after the 1916 Rising, they organised nearly 1,000 young men and women to leave the city to go to Caherdavin, allegedly to watch a GAA match. They returned several hours later and tried to gain access to the city without permits, via Sarsfield Bridge. The soldiers stationed at Shannon rowing club near the bridge fired warning shots, and a tank (nicknamed 'Scotch and Soda') and armoured cars came out and secured the bridge, to prevent them returning. After a tense stand-off the protesters left and took refuge in the houses of Thomandgate and St Munchin's Hall, where they were provided with food and shelter. The next morning they commandeered the Ennis train and returned, unopposed, to Limerick City. The Volunteers had managed to smuggle around 1,000 people into the city without permits, and had fed and sheltered them.[56] On 27 April, following negotiations with local churchmen (mainly Bishop Dr Dennis Hallinan), the Strike Committee issued a proclamation that the strike had ended. In return, the Special Military Area was also terminated. It was reported in the *Limerick Chronicle* on 6 May that, although Limerick was still under martial law, there was free ingress to the city, and permits to enter were no longer required. Barriers and guards at several approaches to the city were removed.

Throughout the day on Thursday 10 April, thousands of people from all over Limerick and the surrounding counties passed by Robert Byrne's coffin, which was lying in state before the high altar in St John's Cathedral. The flag of the town hall flew at half mast and the hundreds of Volunteers present formed a guard of honour. At ten past three, amid immense military presence, the funeral left the Cathedral. Extra RIC and military were on duty on the streets and in reserve in their barracks; armoured cars were positioned at key areas and two aeroplanes circled over St John's Cathedral. The hearse was covered in wreaths and Volunteers carried many more. The *Irish Independent* termed it, 'a most remarkable funeral demonstration'. At least 15,000 mourners must have marched, including the Mayor, Alphonsus O'Mara, and members of the Corporation. The funeral made its way through the old town, the Mall, Patrick Street and William Street, to the cemetery. As it passed military and RIC posts, they presented arms as a mark of respect. The procession was so large it took an hour and ten minutes to pass any given point.[57]

It arrived at Mount St Lawrence cemetery, where Fr Connolly gave the graveside oration.[58] Connie was in the firing party, under the command of Captain Michael McCann of 'D' Company, with Commandant Michael Brennan as director of operations. Normally Connie would have been in charge of the firing parties in Mount St Lawrence, but due to the occasion, that privilege was given to Captain Michael McCann, his superior officer. Patrick and a small party of 'A' Company stood guard over the grave, right up to evening time, and afterwards Patrick returned their weapons to the company arms dump.[59] On 15 July 1919, the widow of Constable O'Brien was awarded £1,200 compensation, for the shooting of her husband in the City Home, by the Ennis County Court Judge, Lord Justice O'Connor.

On 13 September 1919, an article in the *Limerick Chronicle* describes co-ordinated raids in the city:

> Yesterday morning a force of military constabulary, under command of District Inspector Craig, raided some private residences and local clubs in search of arms. Searches were made at the residence of Mr M.P. Colivet MP for the City, Mr Richard P.O. Connor BC, the Catholic Commercial and Professional club, O'Connell Street: the Sinn Féin Registrations office: the Sinn Féin Office, William Street: the Claughaun hurling club, and the Clare Street Workmen's club. No arms were found and no arrests were made. In two or three cases an entrance had to be effected by force, owing to no person being in occupation. Some papers got at Mr Colivet's residence were taken possession of by the constabulary.

Because of several raids like this on his home in the latter part of 1919, Connie was forced to leave Blackboy Pike, after it was raided several times throughout the year by British soldiers and the RIC. This must have been a very stressful time

The remnants of Blackboy Pike, with only the chimney remaining.

for Connie and the McNamara family, especially his younger stepbrothers and sisters. Patrick, the next oldest, was fifteen years old at the time and the youngest, Christopher, was only around six years old, and so it must have been terrifying for them to have armed soldiers coming into their home and ransacking it. In order to protect his home and family, Connie left and was forced to go on the run. Patrick and Thomas remained in the house and looked after the family.[60]

According to my mum, Patsy Corbett, her father spent his time avoiding capture by the British by sleeping in safe houses and graveyards, until his capture in July 1920. As Mount St Lawrence overlooked his house, it must have given him a sense of comfort when he stayed there, knowing he was watching over his family. The stress of being hunted never left him; sometime in the summer of 1954, Connie and his second wife May stayed at a hotel in Crosshaven Co. Cork. For some reason or another, the owner's daughter came into their room in the middle of the night, probably to collect some mislaid belongings, and according to May, as soon as she entered, Connie sat up in bed white as a sheet, and all the hair on his head stood up on end.[61] Clearly those dark days came flooding back the moment the stranger came silently into his room. Capture or assassination were very real concerns for Volunteers and especially those on the run. Connie must have had many sleepless nights during those times.

All Volunteers service was unpaid and members supported themselves with their day jobs, if they had one. Those on the run and those in the Active Service Units and Flying Columns were supported by Volunteer contributions and by the help of the ladies of Cumann na mBan, who would have found them safe houses, food, clothing and the other necessities of life such as cigarettes and the odd drink. Connie, Patrick and Thomas supported their Volunteer activities in their jobs as pork butchers. In the latter part of 1919, in recognition of his services and leadership abilities, Connie was promoted to the rank of captain, and became commanding officer of 'A' Company. He retained this position until the end of the siege of the Strand Barracks in July 1922, when he was imprisoned by Free State forces.[62]

In the area of his command, practically every Loyalist house was raided and every available firearm taken and safely deposited in the company arms dump, to be looked after by Martin Barry. In December 1919, on one of these raids, Connie had a very lucky escape. He had led a small party of 'A' company (including his brother Patrick) on a raid for arms. They raided the home of Colonel Green-Barry, a prominent Loyalist, near Sheehans Cross, Co. Limerick, and were surprised by British military officers who happened to be in residence there. After a twenty-minute firefight, Connie and his men escaped, and just as they fled the scene British reinforcements arrived in lorries.[63]

1920: The Active Service Unit

Throughout Ireland, the attacks on the RIC and the British military started to increase, and some spectacular attacks on RIC barracks took place in the Limerick area. Connie commanded his Active Service Unit throughout his battalion area and neighbouring ones, and occasionally helped Flying Columns in neighbouring counties. During attacks on RIC barracks, they were usually deployed on duties such as the felling of trees, road obstruction and cutting telegraph wires; generally preventing British soldiers from neighbouring garrisons from reaching the main attacking party. They were also used in supplying arms and ammunition to the Flying Columns prior to their attacks, and the removal of the arms afterwards. After such raids, the weapons were returned to the various company ammunition dumps, where Patrick would help strip and clean the weapons, so that they would be ready for the next time they were needed.

Connie used every opportunity to make life difficult for the British, and he was very successful, up until his eventual arrest in July of that year. In early 1920, he organised a highly-mobile cycling corps for the battalion.[64] The RIC also had cycling patrols, which were used to great affect as they could cover a great deal of ground quickly and approach unsuspecting men silently.

On the evening of 24 January, Connie, Patrick and his ASU co-operated with Third Battalion Mid-Limerick Brigade in the attack on Murroe RIC Barracks. About twenty-four men, all from the Murroe–Castleconnell area, in search of guns and ammunition, attacked the barracks. The operation was planned to take place at midnight, under cover of darkness. An early-warning system had been set up, which involved a number of watchmen placed on nearby hills, in Castletroy, Hourigans Hill and Knockbrack Hill. Each group had ten-foot-high post poles, with sods of turf on top of them and with an iron spike soaked in petrol. If there was any movement in the barracks, or any British troop activities in the area, the signal fire was to be lit and passed on, thus giving the attackers time to withdraw. Two sergeants and six RIC policemen were known to be in Murroe Barracks. There were two attacking groups – one to engage the RIC inside the barracks with rifle fire from near the parish church, and the other to bore a hole in the gable end of the barracks in which to place a mine, aimed at blowing a hole in the wall, allowing the Volunteers to enter and get the guns and ammunition.

But they had not calculated the thickness of the walls or the weather. Bill Wall, an explosives expert, was to operate the mine. The problem was digging a hole big enough in which they could place it; at some stage they discovered a big foundation stone and they could go no further. With rain belting down and turning everything to mud, all they could do was to pad the mine with mud and fix it fairly upright, as close as they could get to the gable end.

Bill Wall succeeded in setting a fuse and after one o'clock the mine went off with a huge explosion that was heard miles away. It blew a fairly large hole, but it failed to provide entry. The RIC immediately lit their lamps and sent up flares. In the meantime a signal had been given from Volunteers watching the roads for the attackers to withdraw, and by 2a.m. everyone, including Connie, had withdrawn. Any arms that were taken from the company dumps were returned and cleaned.

Connie and his men had been deployed in the usual way; they had blocked most of the roads with trees and large stones and cut the telegraph wires between Limerick and Nenagh, and those to Dublin. He and his men had built strong barricades, especially at Barrington Bridge, near Boher. The main attacking force surrounded the barracks, and a secondary force blocked the surrounding roads so reinforcements would be delayed. These measures prevented District Inspector Craig and his men (who were coming from Limerick City, about eight miles away) from reaching Murroe until some time later.[65] The Very Revd Canon Dwane, Murroe, condemned the attack at Mass the following Sunday. On 29 March, Judge Piggot of the county court, awarded the Postmaster General four sums (£15, £21 15s 6d, £10 and £30) for damage to telegraph poles and wires in the Castleconnell, Killonan, Park and Boher districts.[66] On 6 September 1920, the abandoned barracks was burned to the ground by the local Volunteers of the Third Battalion. Connie, Patrick and the ASU occasionally held armed raids on Post Office mail in search of certain information when tipped off that it would arrive at a specific post office. This tactic was used to get hold of specific military correspondence or intelligence. These raids frequently yielded important information which was then passed on the battalion I/O.

Connie continued to raid prominent Loyalists' houses, like those of Evans, Curtain, Carson, and Lane, for arms and ammunition. On 27 February, the *Limerick Leader* mentions one of Connie's raids. It reports on the raid on Captain Delmege, who lived in Castlepark, Meelick, Co. Limerick:

Around three or four o'clock the previous morning about twenty armed men entered the property, held up the occupants and made an exhaustive search of the property for firearms, the result of the search is not known but it is reported that seven or eight revolvers, one or two rifles, together with some ammunition were taken.

Delmege was the Grand Jury foreman who seconded a motion to send a donation to the RIC Central Benevolent Fund on behalf of the policemen who died in the Robert Byrne rescue.

On Sunday 7 March, Doon RIC Barracks was surrounded and attacked by Volunteers. The *Limerick Leader* noted the following day that traces of blood were discovered in the vicinity, giving the assumption that some of the attacking Volunteers were wounded. Connie, with assistance from the ASU, again commanded his company (including Patrick) in the felling of trees, cutting of wires and the blocking of roads in the Doon attack. The *Limerick Leader* also reported that:

Telegraphic communication between Fermoy and Limerick was still interrupted on Monday (day of print). Owing to blocking of roads for a considerable area around the barracks people travelling in the district had to reach their destinations by byroads. The cutting of trees, wires and making obstructions must have engaged large numbers of men.[67]

In 9 April 1920, Connie and his ASU burnt the abandoned Blackboy Pike RIC Barracks, which was a few hundred yards from his home. This would have given him a great deal of satisfaction, as this was the barracks that would have organised the raids on his home and that which had made him go on the run. Connie burnt Blackboy Pike Barracks first because it was in his area, just across the road from his house. Then they moved the mile or so down to Ballincurra and burnt the abandoned Ballincurra RIC Barracks. Ballinacura was only partially burnt, but on the evening of 8 November, at around half past eight, smoke was seen pouring from the building and it was completely destroyed by fire. Afterwards, a notice was posted by the British military that five houses in the district would be destroyed as a reprisal; many residents in the area moved their furniture to places of safety as no one was sure which houses would be chosen.[68] Both of these had been small rural barracks, abandoned by the RIC when they moved to larger and more defendable barracks in Limerick.

In early April, 400 such abandoned premises were burned to the ground throughout Ireland. On 7 April, the *Limerick Leader* reported that:

> These barracks were raided by armed men, who removed those in charge, generally relatives of the police or caretakers, to a place of safety before setting them on fire. Under recent rearrangements of the stations many small barracks in isolated districts were closed; the police being concentrated in large centres. In some places the wives and children continued in possession. Bombs and explosives were used, or the floor or furniture saturated with paraffin or petrol and then set alight. Telegraph and telephone wires connecting the police stations were cut in all directions. In no case was any injury to any person recorded.

Also in April, Connie, Patrick and the ASU attacked the RIC barracks in John Street, Limerick. After the attack they carried away several revolvers, which were given to M. Daly and then distributed amongst the Volunteers. This raid was unusual, as John Street was an inner-city barracks and therefore it involved more risk, as reinforcements from neighbouring RIC and military barracks would rapidly come to their aid. The attack was not reported in any of the local newspapers; neither were there any reports of any injuries or deaths on either side. But it was mentioned in both Connie's and Patrick's IRA pension statements. So at the time of writing I am uncertain as to how the revolvers were taken, but I am sure it was done by subterfuge rather than hostile action.

In the early hours of 7 May, Connie also assisted in the burning of the Ballyneety Courthouse, around seven miles from Limerick City. This was an ordinary house converted for petty session requirements (magistrate's court) and situated close to the RIC barracks, which was also possibly abandoned. Both were destroyed in the raid.[69] He used the same principles as with the burning of the police barracks, i.e. taking people to a place of safety. Bombs and explosives were employed in the destruction. Floors and furniture were saturated with paraffin or petrol, before setting the courthouse on fire. He also ensured that the telegraph and telephone wires connecting the courthouse to local police stations or military barracks, were also cut.

On the evening of 27 May, Connie and Patrick co-operated on the attack on Kilmallock RIC Barracks, which was led by Tom Malone aka Sean Ford, together with around 200 Volunteers from East Clare, Cork, Tipperary and, of course, Limerick. Six RIC men were wounded in the night-long battle. The Volunteers broke a hole in the roof from a nearby building and threw petrol into it. The RIC, under Sergeant Tobias O'Sullivan, did not surrender and withdrew to an outhouse. Two RIC men were killed (Sergeant Thomas Kane and Constable Joseph Morton), as was one IRA man, Captain Liam Scully, from Glencar, Co. Kerry. Despite the besieged barracks sending up signals for help during the five-hour gun battle, Connie's actions in cutting cables and wires, guaranteed that it took a considerable time for reinforcements to arrive.[70]

The *Limerick Leader*, 7 June, reported that in the House of Commons, Sir William Davidson asked the Chief Secretary why no assistance had been given to the ten policemen at Killmallock for upwards of five hours, after two of their number had been killed and the west wing of the barracks had been destroyed by fire against a hostile force. The Chief Secretary, Sir Hamar Greenwood, replied that owing to the fact that the roads were blocked and the railways were torn up, a considerable time elapsed before their arrival. Sir Hamar Greenwood mentioned on the previous day, that a coroner was unable to hold an inquest for the dead policemen as, when he summoned a jury, only four men turned up.

Later on in June, Connie stood guard at the home of Captain Michael Hartney, of 'B' Company, in Davis Street, Limerick City. At the time, Hartney's premises had been threatened with attack on a number of occasions by the British, and it was felt it needed the protection of the local Volunteers. As a result, Connie and other Volunteers were assigned to look after it on a rota basis.[71] The premises were eventually destroyed in a bomb attack in July 1920. Hartney later became Mayor of Limerick in 1945-46.

On Monday morning, 11 July, Rearcross RIC Barracks in North Tipperrary was surrounded and attacked. It bordered the territory of the Third Battalion Mid-Limerick Brigade.

So Connie would have assisted the Castleconnell and Murroe Battalion, and also the Sixth Battalion, First Tipperary Brigade, who carried out the main thrust of the five-hour attack. During the attack, RIC Sergeant Stokes was killed and several policemen were wounded. Strangely enough the attack started at 5.00a.m. in broad daylight; owing to this, the Verey lights fired by the police were not seen in the nearby garrison towns. Connie, with assistance from the Active Service Unit, again commanded his company in the felling of trees, cutting of wires and the blocking of roads with stone barricades in the Rearcross attack; but these precautions started the previous Saturday night. The attack was meant to happen on the Saturday evening, but was postponed until the Sunday evening/Monday morning for some unknown reason.[72] In Connie's pension statement he says it was the Newport RIC Barracks that he attacked, when in fact it was the Rearcross Barracks, a few miles away.

Connie was arrested in mid-July 1920 by the RIC, and when they searched him, they found leaflets relating to boycotting the RIC, documents on how to use explosives and instructions as to ambushing police and military. They then removed him to Mount Brown RIC Barracks, near Rathkeale Co. Limerick. This was a temporary military barracks, used at one stage by the Green Howard regiment. His pension statement noted he was 'carried as a hostage' for two weeks by Crown Forces. In effect, he was carried on a lorry in a prominent position where he could be clearly be seen, either tied to a post on the back or strapped on the bonnet and driven around the surrounding area. This was a common practice when the military were on patrol; prominent Republicans were used as a safety precaution against bomb or grenade attack. The British Army in Dublin started carrying captured Sinn Féin TDs tied to posts on their lorries when on patrol to stop grenade attacks on them, with signs saying, 'Bomb us now.' By way of retaliation Michael Collins launched an ambitious plan to kidnap twenty-five MPs in London. For some reason early in 1921, the practice of hostage-taking ceased in Ireland, possibly due to foreign journalists in Dublin giving extensive coverage of this practice. Collins, in turn, then called off the London kidnappings.[73] The British Army later covered their trucks with a mesh to prevent grenade and bomb attacks, to which the IRA responded by attaching hooks to grenades which would catch in the mesh.

The conditions in the Mount Brown Barracks were appalling and inhumane. An MP brought the filthy condition of the cell he was in to the attention of the English Government in the House of Commons. The House of Commons archives show on 15 July, Conservative MP Sir John David Rees stated, 'May I ask the Chief Secretary for Ireland if he has any information with regard to the arrests of armed men in the district of Limerick?' The Speaker of the House replied, 'The Hon. Member has not given notice of that question.' Notice had to be given in the House to allow time for a member to prepare a response. But the question had its desired effect; it subsequently resulted in Connie's removal from Mount Brown and his transfer to Cork Gaol, in early August, 1920. He was taken to Limerick docks and sailed to Queenstown port in Cork, then taken under armed escort to Cork Gaol.

When Connie was in various prisons in Ireland and England, his interests were looked after by Cumann na mBan and the IRPDF who gave his girlfriend Sally Donnelly and his family regular updates about his health and condition. As well as domestic and medical assistance, they also helped in dispatch work; bringing messages and intelligence to where it was needed. In addition, they transferred small arms and ammunition from place to place; it was easier for a woman to do this as British soldiers were not allowed to search females. The committees met weekly to examine reports of all cases, receive collections and, where necessary, to make grants to families of men in prison or on the run. The Sinn Féin clubs also did collections, which they passed on to Cumann na mBan.[74] First aid classes were started under the Department of Education and each member who passed the examination was given a grant. That, in turn, found its way to the Volunteers arms fund; so ironically the British Government was helping to finance the Volunteers in Limerick.

The first Flying Column in Ireland was formed in East Limerick in early June 1920. It was the brainchild of Donnchadha O'Hannigan and Patrick Clancy. The first action of the new column was at Ballynahinch, near Kilfinane, Co. Limerick, in July 1920, when they ambushed and disarmed an RIC patrol going between Elton and Kilfinane. While this was the first Flying Column in Ireland, Connie's pension statement indicates that smaller Active Service Units were operating in and around Limerick prior to that. The Mid-Limerick Brigade Flying Column, which was mainly based around Caherconlish, was formed in late August and Dick O'Connell was its O/C.[75] Its first action was at Ballynagarde where they ambushed an RIC lorry. The RIC lorry escaped, probably due to a breakdown in communications between the Volunteers. After it was formed, one of Connie's Active Service Unit roles was to supply it with weapons prior to attacks and return the weapons to various ammunition dumps afterwards.

While Connie was in Cork Gaol, he was given the prisoner number L722, which he carried with him throughout his prison life. The letter 'L' indicated that he was from Limerick.[76] On 11 August, under prisoners Commandant Con Nunan, he joined a hunger strike against illegal detention. Connie spent eight days on the strike before he started taking food again. In total, there were about sixty prisoners on strike. All the political prisoners went on hunger strike at dinnertime, demanding immediate release. There were only six to eight convicted prisoners; all the remainder were untried prisoners. Others on hunger strike were John Hogan and Michael Fitzgerald of Fermoy, who were arrested eleven months previously without charge, along with Sean Hennessy of Limerick. In the latter stages of the strike the authorities tampered with the water given to prisoners by adding food substances, prompting the prisoners to threaten to refuse water as well. Food was brought into cells and prisoners were bribed to take it. Joseph Murphy of Cork City died on 11 August, after seventy-six days without food. Michael Fitzgerald of Fermoy, Co. Cork, died on 17 October 1920, after sixty-seven days without food. Michael Hennessy of Tullamore, died on 18 October 1920, after sixty-seven days. Arthur Griffith called off the strikes after the death of Terrence Mac Sweeney, the Lord Mayor of Cork on 25 October. Mac Sweeney's strike lasted seventy-four days, before he lapsed into a coma on 20 October. John and Peter Crowley, Thomas Donovan, Michael Burke, Michael O'Reilly, Christopher Upton, John Power, Joseph Kenny and Seán Hennessy, all in Cork Gaol, ended their protest on 12 November 1920.[77] They had been on hunger strike from 11 August; that is ninety-four days without food.

After his hunger strike, Connie was removed from Cork, and escorted under armed guard to Queenstown port and transferred from there with unnamed others to England by a British sloop. Once he was landed on British soil, he was then transferred to Wormwood Scrubbs in West London for a short time. From there was transported around sixty miles to Winchester Prison in Hampshire, near Portsmouth, where he was detained for three weeks.

In September 1920, he was removed from Winchester Prison and taken to Portsmouth docks, around thirty miles away. Here he was put on a ship, transported to Queenstown port, and then brought back to Cork Detention Barracks. On 16 September, he and others were taken to the Queen Victoria Barracks (Collins Barracks), Cork, for their courts martial. The *Limerick Leader* of 17 September reported that in his court martial case on the previous day, a police witness confirmed the documents that Connie was caught in possession of. Connie refused to recognise the court. The Sinn Féin courts were the only courts recognised by the people as a whole; they refused to recognise the British legal system and generally avoided taking their disputes to British courts. Afterwards, he was tried and sentenced to six months imprisonment which was a mild sentence considering the documents he was caught in possession of.[78] When the sentence was passed, he was once again escorted to Queenstown port and transported to Birmingham Prison, where he served his time.

On 10 December 1920, Lord French, the Lord Lieutenant of Ireland, issued a proclamation imposing martial law on the counties of Cork, Kerry, Tipperary and Limerick. Later, on 30 December, this was extended to Kilkenny, Clare, Wexford and Waterford. The British military now had the power to execute anyone found carrying arms and ammunition, or using British uniforms, to search houses, impose curfews, try suspects in military rather than civilian courts, and to intern suspects without trial.[79]

I have only given a brief account of Connie's military operations, based on the information available in his, Patrick's and Thomas' IRA pension statements, their War of Independence Medal statements and various IRA Second Battalion statements. Connie was engaged in many minor activities throughout his area, and there were probably numerous incidents he was involved in which were not documented. Any records related to his activities were committed to memory and quickly destroyed as a measure of protection; being caught with incriminating documents had landed him in prison already, so he ensured he would not be caught with incriminating documents again.[80] In addition to military work, he would have assisted in the maintenance of law and order. Military and Sinn Féin courts were now being used by the population at large because no one wanted to use the British court system. Connie and 'A' Company would have been used to maintain law and order, by supporting the Irish Republican Police in his company area.[81] As this was an unwelcome distraction from their military activities, any crime would have been dealt with quickly and firmly.

1921: The Truce

In early January 1921, the arms dump of the Mid-Limerick Brigade was discovered in a vault in the Inch St Lawrence grave-yard in Caherconlish, Co. Limerick, by the RIC. It was found by accident, by a Black and Tan who was prowling around the graveyard, and who spotted the arms through a light chink in the side of the vault.[82] This was a huge blow to the brigade, severely depleting their arms and ability to launch attacks. The RIC based in Pallas, Co. Tipperary were responsible for the raid.

In response to this attack, a joint operation between the East and Mid-Limerick Brigades was planned, to ambush a convoy of lorries that regularly travelled from Pallas to Fedamore and then returned the same day. The two Flying Columns decided to ambush it on the return leg at Dromkeen; this ambush was to cause the highest loss of life of Crown Forces in Limerick during the War of Independence. Patrick McNamara, along with his comrades in 'A' Company, carried arms to the ambush site and then helped to block the roads leading to the scene in the usual manner. On 3 February, at around 2.30p.m., two lorries were fired upon, and out of a total number of thirteen policemen, eleven were killed. The only Volunteer casualty was Liam Hayes of the East Limerick Brigade, who was shot in the hand. The eleven policemen killed were Samuel Adams, George Bell, John Bourke, Michael Doyle, Patrick Foody, William Hayton, William Kingston, Sidney Millin, Bernard Mollaghan, Arthur Pearce and Henry Smith. District Inspector Sampson and John Cox, one of the drivers, escaped uninjured, aided in that they were the only members of the Column wearing civilian clothing. In response to this attack the British military blocked all access to Limerick City and prevented anyone entering or leaving the city for a number of days afterwards. They also burned about eight houses in retaliation.[83]

Connie was released from Birmingham Prison later in February 1921, and was ferried back to Limerick docks. Soon after he landed, he reported for duty and joined up with 'A' Company again. Taking up from where he left off, he was in charge of an attack with 'A' Company on a regular RIC patrol in Ellen Street, having waited three weeks before eventually ambushing them. This was a regular RIC Column that patrolled Ellen Street every Sunday between 11.00a.m. and 1.00p.m.[84] There are no known records of any deaths or serious injuries on either side.

The following month Connie was arrested, court-martialled and indefinitely interned under DORA, and sent to Spike Island for internment.[85] They sailed from Limerick docks and landed at Queenstown, Co. Cork, and then transferred to Spike Island. The decision to send the men by water rather than overland was a precautionary one, as a journey of some sixty miles through some perfect ambush country was deemed far too dangerous. While Connie was in Spike Island, the prisoners' commanding officers were Commandant Henry O'Mahoney, Vice-Commandant Liam Burke and Adjutant Peadar O'Donnell.[86]

During March 1921, the Volunteers were organised along divisional lines, Connie and the Mid-Limerick Brigade became part of the Second Southern Division, along with the Kilkenny Brigade, East Limerick Brigade, First Tipperary Brigade, Second Tipperary Brigade, Third 'South' Tipperary Brigade, and the North Tipperary Brigade, under the command of Ernie O'Malley. A further result of this reorganisa-

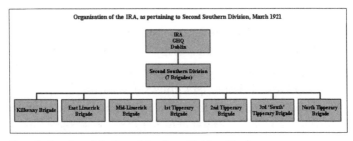

Organisation plan of the Second Southern Division, March 1921.

tion was that the First and the Second Battalions merged and operated as one. Unfortunately this did not put an end to the bitterness between the two battalions, which continued right up to the end of the Civil War.[87]

Early in March, the British arrested the brigade Vice-Commandant Michael Colivet and Captain Micheal Hartney and held them in the Ordnance Barracks, next door to Shaw's bacon factory in Mulgrave Street. They were being forced to accompany British patrols as hostages. The Mid-Limerick Brigade felt that their lives were in danger, as plans were being made to intensify attacks on British patrols and convoys. Brigade Commandant Peadar Dunne then made a plan to rescue them by tunnelling through to their cells from the adjacent bacon factory. Second Battalion O/Cs David Dundon, Robert De Courcy, John Grant, and Paddy Barry were in charge of the operation. On 13 March, at around 7.00a.m., after the staff in Shaw's had been locked in the boilerhouse, Patrick, together with others from 'A' and 'C' Companies, started tunnelling. At about 1.00p.m., after about six hours of tunnelling and just as they nearly reached the prisoners, an armoured car and several lorries of British troops arrived suddenly and set up a cordon in the area around the barracks. The plan had to be called off immediately and the men were very lucky to escape, as they

were practically surrounded by British Infantry. Patrick slipped
through the military cordon and arranged for the weapons
and equipment to be safely brought back to the arms dump
in Lawlor's field.[88] Later on that month, brigade Commandant
Peadar Dunne was arrested by Crown Forces, and Liam Forde
became Commandant of the Mid-Limerick Brigade.

On 1 April 1921, as recognition of his services and ability, Patrick was promoted to section leader in 'A' Company,
under the command of Terence Casey. On 9 April 1921, as a
reprisal for previous attacks, the British Army selected houses
in Lock Quay belonging to prominent IRA officers in prison,
for destruction. McInerney's public house, at nos. 9 and 10
Lock Quay, was blown up. Afterwards, a Crossley tender full
of Black and Tans took the opportunity to avail themselves
of the free drink into the early hours of the morning, before
setting what was left of the building on fire.[89] The premises
was owned by Captain Tommy McInerney of 'C' Company;
he was the transport officer of the Mid-Limerick Brigade
who was in Spike Island with Connie at the time. He was
also the driver of the car that went over Ballykissane Pier in
Holy Week, April 1916.

Records from the British headquarters of the Sixth Division,
Seventeenth Infantry Brigade Cork show that on 3 June 1921,
some thirteen prisoners (including Connie, aka prisoner number
L722, and Tommy McInerney), were taken from Spike Island
by launch and landed at Custom House Quay, Queenstown
port. They were then taken under armed guard by soldiers
of the Seventeenth Infantry Brigade, to Cork Male Gaol. On
Thursday 9 June, Connie and twenty-two others including
Tommy McInerney, were escorted by the Seventeenth Infantry
Brigade and put aboard a War Department boat and the barge

Shannon at Custom House Quay and returned to Spike Island.[90] Tom Malone (alias Sean Ford), Con Twoomey and Sean Mac Sweeney (brother of Terrence Mac Sweeney, the Lord Mayor of Cork) escaped from Spike Island on 29 April. Connie was sent with Captain Tommy McInerney and others to Maryborough Convict Prison (Portlaoise) in late June 1921.[91]

Meanwhile, as Connie was in prison, the Truce of 11 July 1921 was declared, resulting in the ending of all Volunteer hostilities. Negotiations, however, had been delayed since December 1920, as the British Government insisted that the IRA first decommission its weapons, but this demand was eventually dropped. It was agreed that British troops would remain confined to their barracks.[92] Initally de Valera had headed the delegations at the early part of the negotiations. Then on 7 October 1921, de Valera nominated a team of delegates headed by Arthur Griffith, with Michael Collins as his deputy, members Robert Barton, Eamon Duggan and George Duffy, and with Erskine Childers as secretary general. With heavy misgivings, believing de Valera should head the delegation, Collins agreed to go to London. On 11 October 1921, the delegates set up headquarters at 22 Hans Place in Knightsbridge, and resided there until conclusion of the negotiations in December. The negotiations ultimately resulted in the Anglo-Irish Treaty, which was signed on 6 December 1921, and which provided for a new Irish State, named the 'Irish Free State', a literal translation from the Irish Language term Saorstát Éireann. (This, incidentally, appeared on de Valera's letterhead, though he had translated it less literally as the 'Irish Republic'.) The Treaty provided for a possible All-Ireland State, subject to the right of a six-county region in the north-east to opt out of the Free State (which it immediately did). Should this happened, an Irish Boundary Commission was to be established to redraw the Irish border, which Collins expected would so reduce the size of Northern Ireland as to make it economically unviable, thus enabling unity, as most of the Unionist population was concentrated in a relatively small area in eastern Ulster.[93]

On 9 December Connie was released under a general amnesty from Maryborough Convict Prison. All prisoners of a political nature were released from prison around December. On his return to Limerick, Connie reported for duty to his battalion O/C David Dundon. In late December 1921, Connie was again appointed to take command of 'A' company. He, along with Patrick and chosen members of 'A' Company, raided the premises of a Mr Hannigan, in William Lane. Hannigan was not there at the time and they captured an ammunition dump of eight rifles and twelve revolvers, plus grenades and several shotguns.[94] This raid took place during the Truce period and was a blatant breaking of it. Most IRA officers on the ground interpreted the Truce merely as a temporary respite and continued recruiting, training, and also raiding for arms. Nor had attacks on the RIC or British Army ceased altogether. Between December 1921 and February 1922, there were eighty recorded attacks by the IRA on the soon-to-be-disbanded RIC, leaving twelve dead. On 18 February 1922, Ernie O'Malley's IRA unit raided the RIC barracks at Clonmel, taking forty policemen prisoner and seizing over 600 weapons and thousands of rounds of ammunition.[95] The continuing militancy of many IRA leaders was one of the main factors in the outbreak of the Irish Civil War, as they refused to accept the Anglo-Irish Treaty that had been negotiated by Michael Collins and Arthur Griffith.

During the Truce, GHQ issued orders that training camps should be established to perfect the various skills and overall professionalism of the IRA. General Sir Neville Macready, the commander-in-chief of the British forces in Ireland, complained that the Truce was being taken advantage of, to transform 'a disorganised rabble into a well-disciplined and well-armed force'. The truth was, the IRA was weeks away from disaster; they were running out of ammunition and weapons. The Truce gave them the breathing space they needed to regroup and rearm. During the New Year period, Connie was drilling and holding regular parades with his men. He believed that they would soon go into action again and he wanted them to be fully prepared.[96]

Cumann na mBan changed their constitution during the Truce and arranged for more active co-operation with the IRA. Every branch appointed a captain who was specially trained in the use of arms. They regularly recieved bundles of posters, leaflets and other literature from headquarters, and these were then distributed by the members of each district. They were posted on walls and put on chapel gates. Reports on British atrocities were sent abroad to people who could publicise them; they were sent to public figures and newspapers, to embassies and organisations in Britain, and also to gaols, Flying Columns and Active Service Units.[97] After the Treaty was signed the majority of the ladies stayed on the Republican side. During the Civil War the Republician forces were helped in many ways by the gallant ladies of Cumann na mBan, in tending the wounded, ferrying messages and so forth. The wife of Captain Hartney was shot in Adare in August 1922, by Free State forces while she was helping her husband. She was the only member of Cumann na mBan to be killed in action during the War of Independence and the Civil War.[98]

1922: The Civil War

On 3 January 1922, the Republican newspaper *Phoblacht na hÉireann* was published, launched by Liam Mellows, Frank Gallagher and Erskine Childers, who were opposed to the Treaty. Its editorial committee included Republicans Cathal Brugha and Erskine Childers, and it was issued at a time when all the national daily papers were in favour of the Treaty. It presented the views of the Republican leadership, unlike most of the other newspapers of the time. It was later to provide a startling insight into the trials that Connie had to endure for his beliefs. On 20 May, Collins secured a compromise with de Valera – 'the pact' – whereby the two factions of Sinn Féin (Pro- and Anti-Treaty) would fight the Free State's first election jointly and form a coalition government.

After the collapse of the Collins–de Valera pact of 14 June 1922, and the outbreak of the Civil War on 28 June, Childers joined the IRA as a Staff-Captain, but confined himself to propaganda issues, to which he was most suited. Childers was constantly hunted by the Free State forces and he secretly ran a mobile printing press along the Cork–Kerry border, moving it along on a horse and cart. This was a remarkable feat in itself given the difficulties in dismantling and reassembling a printing press when moving from place to place. Also, paper was very difficult to obtain. Nevertheless, he was able to produce 20,000 copies of *Phoblacht na hÉireann* every week, sending it to embassies, newspapers, gaols and beyond. He was arrested on 10 November, in Annamoe, Co. Wicklow, at the house of his cousin Robert Barton. Childers was executed on 24 November 1922, by a Free State firing squad in Portabello Barracks (Cathal Brugha Barracks). With his death, the IRA lost one of its most effective propagandists and it also meant the end of *Phoblacht na hÉireann*, the mouthpiece of the Republican forces.[99]

The British forces started to withdraw from Limerick early in the New Year of 1922. The process started in late February and was completed by 25 March. The last battalion to leave the Strand Barracks was the First Battalion of Oxford and Buckinghamshire Light Infantry, who handed it over to the Free State.[100] The barracks was later handed over to the Republican forces by an arrangement made with the provisional government and General Liam Lynch, O/C Second Southern Division. Collins was quite alarmed at what was happening in Limerick and tried in vain to get Winston Churchill to postpone the evacuation of British troops there. But Churchill was only too happy to get his troops out of Limerick, rather than leaving them in a Republican heartland in an already worsening situation.

On 18 February 1922, Liam Ford, Commandant of the Mid-Limerick Brigade, issued a proclamation, 'We no longer recognise the authority of the present head of the army, and renew our allegiance to the existing Irish Republic.' This, in effect, threw down the gauntlet to the Free State, thereby committing Connie and his men to the Republican side and against the newly formed Free State Government.

The government then ordered Michael Brennan, Commandant General of the Pro-Treaty First Western Division forces, into Limerick to take over positions evacuated by the British on 23 February. In turn, the Anti-Treaty Divisional Commandant for the Second Southern Division, Ernie

O'Malley, sent troops into Limerick. He also sent for seventy men from the Second Southern Division in Tipperary, hoping to be able to capture the Strand Barracks and King John's Castle with this force. Unable to do so, his men occupied a number of hotels in the city instead, with O'Malley making the Glentworth Hotel his headquarters. There were now three armed groups in Limerick. Ernie O'Malley and his men occupied several prominent buildings in the city. Brennan was in control of some newly evacuated British positions and there were still two fully armed battalions of British troops in the city.[101] The situation was very tense in Limerick and it looked like an armed clash might break out at any moment between the two Irish forces, which could escalate into Civil War.

The Mayor of Limerick, Stephen O'Mara, traveled to Dublin to negotiate a settlement and on 5 March a compromise was reached. The terms were that the police barracks were to be held by the Limerick Corporation, outside troops were to return to their own areas, and a small maintenance party of local troops under Lynch's authority were to occupy the military barracks. The Pro-Treaty IRA was unhappy with the compromise as they saw it as a climbdown. Anti-Treaty IRA was equally unhappy, as they saw their numeric advantage nullified by a truce that did them no favours.[102]

On 11 March Liam Lynch agreed the Truce. This resulted in postponing the battle for Limerick until July, and gave the Free State troops the breathing space they needed to regroup, rearm and more importantly, to be reinforced. As a result of the Truce, Connie was then commanded by Lynch to take over the Ordnance Barracks in Mulgrave Street from the Free State forces under the command of Commandant General Michael Brennan. Once he had done so, he installed a training regime for the men to prepare them for the oncoming battle, and arranged for them to make explosives.

Once the Ordnance Barracks was safely secured and firmly under Republican control, with the men fully trained and ready, Connie (along with Captain Henry Meaney), was ordered to take command of the Castle Barracks, which were again under the command of Commandant General Michael Brennan. Once more, he installed a training regime for the men, preparing them for what was to come. For a short period Patrick was assigned to the Republican garrison in St Joseph's mental institution, which was just beside Limerick Prison in Mulgrave Street. Then he was reassigned to the Ordnance Barracks and promoted to acting Orderly Sergeant, until he was transferred to Red Cross duty. He remained in the barracks until it was evacuated in July. Thomas McNamara was also stationed at the Ordnance Barracks but his duties were not documented.[103]

Around the end of March 1922, Connie was appointed to command the Strand Barracks. Thomas was assigned there at this time also.[104] The strength of the barracks varied at times from thirty to one hundred men, and consisted of men from the East and West Limerick Brigades, as well as Connie's own Mid-Limerick Brigade of the Republican forces. This was the only barracks on the Clare side of the River Shannon and it was the one that was to take the most punishment from the Free State forces. It also was the barracks that put up the stiffest resistance.[105]

On the morning of 13 April 1922, Anti-Treaty men of the First Dublin Brigade, acting on orders from the Army Council, occupied the Four Courts as Republican headquarters, and other prominent buildings in Dublin, to pressurise

Right: Patrick and his men photographed in the Ordnance Barracks.

Below: Connie inside the main gate of the Ordnance Barracks after the handover by Michael Brennan.

An 18-pounder gun in Hammond Lane, Dublin, aimed at the Four Courts, shortly before shelling commenced on 28 June. (*Image courtesy of the National Library of Ireland.*)

Dáil Éireann and the Provisional Government of the Irish Free State to return to war with Britain. Stalemate ensued until 28 June, when the Irish Free State Army was put under pressure from Britain to retake the Four Courts.[106] This was due to the assassination of Sir Henry Wilson, a retired British Field Marshal, on 22 June. Sir Henry was the military advisor to the Northern Ireland Government and he was assassinated, allegedly, on Collins' orders, in retaliation for the widespread anti-Catholic atrocities in the North. Orange mobs regularly attacked Catholic areas with the collusion of the newly formed RUC. There were widespread murders and evictions and some Catholic communities in Belfast were virtually under siege.[107]

On 28 June, the Free State began shelling the Four Courts. These opening shots were to pit brother against brother, friend against friend, and neighbour against neighbour. This

Assistant Chief of Staff General Eoin O'Duffy, Commandant General Mick
Brennan, and Commandant General W.R.E. Murphy during the Irish Civil War.
(*Image courtesy of the National Library of Ireland.*)

was the start of the Civil War. The first shots fired from the
18-pounder pieces of British Army artillery were from the
junction of Bridgefoot Street and Usher's Quay. One of these
same pieces would later visit the Strand Barracks and give
Connie quite a bit of discomfort.

The operation was under the command of Emmet Dalton
and Tom Ennis, who had called for the Republican forces in
the Four Courts to surrender, which they refused to do. The
first shots fired did not hit their target but, ironically, landed
in the headquarters of General Macready, from where the
guns had been borrowed. The bombardment continued every
fifteen minutes for three days.[108]

On 29 June, at the request of the commandant of the Four
Courts garrison, Rory O'Connor, *Phoblacht na hÉireann* published a proclamation from the Irregular troops entrenched
within the Four Courts, to their former comrades now shell-

ing them, 'We especially appeal to our former comrades of the Irish Republic to return to that allegiance and thus guard the nation's honour from the infamous stigma that her sons aided her foes in returning a hateful domination over her.' Despite the appeal, the Free State gunners continued the bombardment, and the Four Courts garrison surrendered the following day, on 30 June. After its fall, control of Limerick became vital; whoever controlled Limerick also controlled the Shannon Bridges commanding the South and West, the gateway to Cork and Kerry. At the time Limerick was occupied by both Free State and Republican troops, who raced to take control of the city. With the capture of chief of staff Joe McKelvey at the Four Courts, Liam Lynch resumed the position of chief of staff of Republican forces, and established his headquarters in the New Barracks in Limerick on 29 June.[109]

The Republican forces intended to set up a Munster Republic by organising a defensive fortified line between Limerick and Waterford. Liam Lynch hoped to use this Munster Republic as a bargaining chip to renegotiate the Treaty. Despite having the advantage over the Free State both in terms of men and weapons, they chose an indecisive defensive option, rather than an aggressive one which would have suited their men better. Most of the more experienced Volunteers had taken the Republican side and the Free State Army was made up mostly of inexperienced recruits. But, as the conflict grew, the Free State went on a massive recruitment drive and was supplied with a large amount of arms and equipment such as artillery and armored cars by the British. On the other hand, the only sources of arms that the Republican side had were those captured from the Free State and weapons handed over by sympathetic Free State troops.[110] Funding also became difficult for the Republican side and they had to turn to bank raids to finance themselves, whereas the Free State was being bankrolled by the British Treasury. Public support also turned against them; as Harry Boland stated, 'There is no doubt that the people in the main are against us, believing that we are to blame for the present state of affairs.'

On 20 May 1922, Collins secured a compromise with de Valera, whereby the two factions of Sinn Féin (Pro- and Anti-Treaty) would fight the Free State's first election jointly and form a coalition government afterwards. Many on the Republican side were unhappy with it, as they saw it as an attempt to mislead them, but both Collins and de Valera signed it as a last ditch attempt to control events. On 14 June, the Collins–de Valera pact of 20 May broke down, when Collins rejected the pact and told an audience in Cork that they, 'must vote for the best candidate ... the country must have the representatives it wants. You understand fully what you have to do and I depend on you to do it.'[111]

On 16 June, the general election was held in the twenty-six counties. The Free State constitution appeared in the papers on the morning of polling day, and it was a disappointment to Republicans who alleged it was deliberately delayed. The real issue of the election was not the constitution, but rather whether the Treaty was acceptable to the people of Ireland or not. On 24 June, the election results became known; it had been won by the Pro-Treaty Faction, although they did not have a clear majority. Pro-Treaty votes were 239,193 out of 620,283 cast; the Anti-Treaty vote was 133,864, and the Independents and Farmers, 247,226. Although both sides admitted it was a vote for peace, it did not prevent the terrible chain of events that were to follow.[112]

On 4 July, Commandant General Michael Brennan, in order to stall for time to obtain reinforcements and to get his men into more strategic positions, arranged a truce in Limerick between himself and Liam Lynch. He had no intention of keeping it; Lynch however was duped into thinking that Brennan's position was much stronger than it actually was. Lynch not only kept the Truce but also kept all his men in Limerick. The delay allowed the Free State forces to build up their strength while also having a demoralising effect on the Republican forces. Moreover, the Free State GHQ had doubts about Brennan's loyalty for agreeing to the Truce. On 7 July, despite efforts on both sides, fighting broke out in Limerick between Free State and Republican forces. There were no reported casualties but in order to stop the hostilities escalating, another truce was agreed.[113]

Beginning on July 10, Republican prisoners were released, on signing a pledge not to take up arms again against the provisional government. This was mainly because the Free State did not have the facilities to cope with the large numbers of Republican prisoners. This 'pledge' was available throughout the Civil War. Although a few took advantage of it in order to gain their freedom, the majority, like Connie, chose to endure their hardships rather than to sign away their principles.[114] The long-awaited Free State arms consignment arrived in Limerick, via Galway and Clare, from Dublin on 11 July, along with 150 troops. By 5.00p.m. on 11 July, Free State forces, now fully armed, were advancing to new positions in the city. Private O'Brien, a Free State soldier, was shot in the back as he was erecting a barricade in Nelson (Parnell) Street. Brennan then sent Lynch formal confirmation that the Truce was over, using the shooting of O'Brien as a pretext to end the Truce.

At 7.00p.m. hostilities commenced when Free State troops, at a position in William Street, opened fire on the Ordnance Barracks, where Patrick was stationed.[115]

William Street served as the Free State's front line, with buildings on each side of it held by opposing troops. The Republicans were in control of the majority of the city located south of this position. The government position on William Street was centred on the RIC barracks, with strong points north of this position in the custom house and the courthouse. Further north, however, the Republicans occupied Castle Barracks, located next to the thirteenth-century King John's Castle, as well as the Strand Barracks across the River Shannon. Streets were barricaded and snipers shot from upper-floor windows. Many of the buildings in the city were connected by tunnels, and these were used by both sides.

The fighting largely consisted of small-scale sallies made by both sides against their opponent's strong points. Needless to say, it was the civilians who suffered the worst: business was brought to a standstill and food became very scarce, almost to the point of famine. Neither did it help that Republican forces had taken over the bacon factories in the city. As the *Old Limerick Journal* stated, 'in a city that had four bacon factories, rashers became rare as rubies'. Both sides tried to ease the hardship by suppling food to the populace but, as in any war, the soldiers get fed first and the little that was left over was not sufficient to look after the needs of the local people. Getting about their daily business became a dangerous task for the ordinary Limerick citizens, with edgy snipers shooting at anything that moved. Profiteering and looting was also taking place, but when discovered, perpitrators were dealt with harshly by both sides.[116]

By 12 July, with fighting underway in Limerick, Lynch realised how vulnerable his headquarters was. In order to safeguard it, he left the city and strategically transferred his headquarters to the more secure town of Clonmel, where he was later joined by de Valera. Had he not done so, some enterprising Free State officer might have decided to try to end the War in one fell swoop, by capturing his headquarters and possibly, the Republican chief of staff, as had happened to the whole Free State Brigade staff in East Limerick on the same day. In that incident, forty-seven men were captured by the Republicans and taken to Tipperary Barracks. Later that afternoon, Free State troops launched an attack in Limerick City, capturing a Republican outpost and thirteen men.[117]

On Thursday 13 July, in response to the previous day's attack, Republican forces in the Ordnance Barracks ordered Patrick McNamara and other Volunteers to launch an attack on the nearby Free State position in Munster Fair Tavern, on Mulgrave Street, which they captured and held briefly. The Free State troops responded swiftly by launching an all-out counter-attack. Their armoured cars smashed their way through the barricades in Mulgrave Street and advanced as far as the walls of the Ordnance Barracks, where they made an attempt to mine them, but were driven off by the furious defence of the men within. They did, however, retake the Munster Fair Tavern in the attack and Patrick and his associates retreated to the safety of the Ordnance Barracks.[118] The Free State forces now turned their full attention to the Strand Barracks.

The Strand Barracks

The Free State forces were now controlling three of the four bridges leading into Limerick City; only Thomond Bridge was held by the Republicans. Both the Castle and Strand Barracks were isolated from the rest of the Republican forces in Limerick City. Connie had the Free State forces controlling Sarsfield Bridge on his right flank and across the river on Arthur's Quay, leaving only his rear and Thomand Bridge (on his left flank) free. But troops were slowly advancing to his rear, towards the Castle Barracks and Thomand Bridge. Soon he and his men would be completely surrounded.[119]

Since the end of March, when Connie had taken command of the Strand Barracks, he had been preparing it for the inevitable conflict. He had surrounded several RIC barracks in his time with the ASU, so he knew which strategy the Free State troops would use to attack him and how he should prepare for the inevitable assault. The only difference now was that they would be attacking a position that was expecting them and was fully prepared. Connie had organised the men within the barracks into different squadrons and had ensured that the provisions were fully stocked.[120] As the situation in Limerick steadily worsened, a Red Cross field hospital was established beside the barracks, in preparation for the care of the wounded in the oncoming conflict. There were an estimated sixty-five men there at this stage. Thanks to Connie's foresight, they had managed to stockpile a huge amount of food, cigarettes, and most importantly, ammunition. With these supplies, they could hold out for a considerable time.

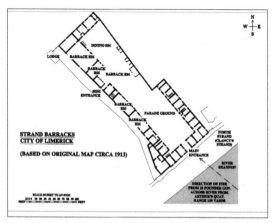

Plan of the Strand Barracks, taken from 1913 originals.

On the evening of Saturday 15 July, an all-out attack was launched on Republican positions in both the Strand Barracks and Castle Barracks, involving armoured cars, grenades, machine guns and mortar fire. Armoured cars charged down Clancy's Strand under covering fire from across the river on Arthur's Quay. The attacks were beaten back from behind the four-foot thick barrack walls, and the Free State troops had to retreat and regroup to plan their next move. The thick walls of the Strand Barracks could only be breached by the use of artillery, a conclusion eventually reached by the Free State GHQ. The Free State forces were now running short of ammunition and were desperate to be resupplied. Later on that day, Liam Lynch moved his headquaters fifteen miles inland from Clonmel to Fermoy, Co. Cork, even further away from the pitched battle that was taking place in Limerick City. On Sunday, another onslaught was launched on the Strand Barracks, which left the East wing in flames. Connie and his men retreated to other parts of the barracks and continued their valiant defence.[121]

On Monday 17, assistant chief of staff General Eoin O'Duffy left Dublin to assume personal control of operations in Limerick and the other counties in the Munster Republic. He brought along a convoy under Commandant Denis Galvin that included a Whippet armoured car, 2 Lancia armoured cars, 4 trucks carrying troops, 400 rifles with 40,000 rounds, 10 Lewis guns with 10,000 rounds, 400 grenades, and, most important of all, an 18-pounder field gun. General O'Duffy established his headquarters north of Limerick in Killaloe.[122]

Now that they had been alerted to the imminent arrival of substantial Free State reinforcements, the Republican forces launched an all-out attack on Tuesday 18 July, in an effort to drive their enemies out of Limerick. Despite suffering substantial casualties, the Free State troops held their ground. Aware of the dangers, Mayor Stephen O'Mara asked the civilians to evacuate places near the Strand and Castle Barracks because of the danger of artillery fire.

Thousands of refugees fled the city as soon as they saw the artillery coming and took refuge in the surrounding townlands of Clarina, Adare and even as far as the town of Nenagh in Co. Tipperary.[123] Connie ordered Thomas to leave the Strand Barracks, as he had enough to worry about at that time and did not need the extra worry of his younger brother facing the newly arrived 18-pounder. It is not documented what happened to Thomas, but he was probably captured by Free State troops soon after. Thomas states in his application for a Volunteer Special Allowance that he was 'offered encouragement' to join the Free State side. I take this to mean that after he was captured he was offered a bribe, which he refused. Many Volunteers were offered a house and a steady income to join the Free State side. This was an attractive proposal for the poor working man; times were hard and work was scarce. Thomas McNamara used to say to his son Brendan, years later, that many of the men 'changed their collars', i.e. went from the folded-down collar of the Volunteer uniform to the standing collar of the Free State uniform.

The Free State ship SS *Arvonia* landed in Limerick docks, bringing a number of troops, equipment and supplies, which were speedily dispatched to key areas. Thus, more and more troops were brought against the hopelessly outnumbered Republican forces. The Republican troops in the Castle Barracks realised that their position was soon to be overrun and they would have to either retreat or surrender. It was decided that as many fighting men as possible were to be smuggled in a Red Cross ambulance from the Castle Barracks to the Strand Barracks. After several journeys, the Free State troops realised what was happening and opened fire on the ambulance to the horror of watching citizens, who thought that a terrible atrocity was taking place.[124] The Free State troops had now started to move to the rear of Connie's Company, leaving only Thomand Bridge and the Castle Barracks in Republican hands, preventing a complete encirclement.

On Wednesday 19 July, an early-morning attack by Free State forces in massed formation was launched against the rear of the Strand Barracks in an attempt to lay a mine. The intention was to breach the rear of the barracks. They were led by armoured cars and were further covered by machine-gun and mortar fire. But, after a lengthy battle, they were driven off by accurate fire from Connie and his men.[125] *Phoblacht na hÉireann*, on 22 July, belatedly reported this attack, 'The Strand Barracks "although practically surrounded, are making a gallant defence". An attempt to lay a mine at the rear of the position was defeated by accurate fire.'

During the previous days, the garrison in the Strand Barracks was subject to constant attacks from the Free State troops. These constant attacks were supported by heavy machine-gun fire, frequent sniping, mortar fire, and charges by armoured cars (including the Whippet armoured car 'Danny Boy'), which had left the front entrance in a demolished state.[126] During a lull in the fighting, barricades were speedily erected again, putting the barracks back in a sound state of defence. As soon as they had been replaced, fighting resumed. There was constant rattle of sniper and mortar fire, day and night, giving Connie and his men little time for rest.[127]

On Thursday 20 July, the Free State forces mounted yet another early-morning assault at the rear of the barracks, led once more by armoured cars, under furious covering fire by mortars and machine guns. This was another desperate attempt to capture the barracks, but the fierce resistance of Connie and his men not only drove their enemies back, but even managed to knock out an armoured car.[128] Up to this point, all efforts to capture the barracks had failed, and so the Free State troops were getting impatient. They had clearly not expected this level of resistance. They now decided to use their artillery piece on the Strand, to move these diehards out of the barracks once and for all. At 10.00a.m., a Republican prisoner with a white flag brought a message to Connie from Commandant General Brennan. He was given an ultimatum; the barracks was to be shelled by the 18-pounder artillery gun and if he did not surrender within five minutes, Connie would be responsible for all loss of life. Unfortunately, as the prisoner was talking to Connie, he was shot and badly wounded by a Republican sniper from another position. Connie steadfastly refused to accept these conditions and sent two nurses with

The Strand
Barracks as it is
today; the red-
bricked house
on the right,
'Conakeane', still
has the bullet holes
from the siege.

a white flag from the Red Cross hospital beside the barracks, replying, 'he would not surrender while he had still had
ammunition or cover'.[129]

The shelling of the barracks commenced soon afterwards.
Incidentally, the field gun was one of those used to bombard
the Four Courts a few weeks previously. However, the Free
State gunners had no training on how to use it. Also, the gun
had no sights, so the only way the gunners had of aiming,
was to look down the barrel, roughly guess the range and
direction, and then fire. The shells were solid, as they were
not given high explosive ones by the British.

The 18-pounder was positioned on Arthur's Quay, not far
from the city courthouse, about 150 yards across the Shannon.
They fired at point-blank range, with everything they had,
including rifles and heavy machine guns. The bullet holes
can still be seen on neighbouring houses, especially on the
Georgian house called 'Conakeane', to the immediate right
of the barracks. The *New York Times* reported that Connie's
men tunnelled into the house in the defence of the barracks,

which is why it is so badly riddled. 'Conakeane' is now a listed building and the outside walls, where the bullet marks are still to be seen, cannot be interfered with.

The bombardment lasted for several hours, until the barracks' four-foot-thick front walls had been breached where the nineteen shells fired had made a huge hole. The *Limerick Leader* reported, 'the front gate was blown away with a shell and two large holes forged in the masonry work, one of which was sufficient to admit a horse and cart to pass through'. Soon, all entrances by the front gate had to be abandoned. The men had to move deeper within the barracks for better cover; to have stayed close to the front under this furious bombardment would have meant certain death. Even though they were under constant attack day and night, and had been through a terrifying artillery bombardment, they still refused to surrender. In fact, they were replacing the barricades and strengthening their defences as best they could.[130]

With the men in the Strand still resisting, the Free State forces then moved the 18-pounder gun across Sarsfield Bridge, to the rear of the barracks. Fourteen more shells were fired and the building was breached by 8.00p.m. Still, the brave men inside refused to surrender. Meanwhile, the Republicans in the city had launched a major attack to rescue the Strand Barracks. Their advance up O'Connell Street, however, was caught in the crossfire of machine gun bullets coming from Free State positions at the ends of Thomas Street and William Street, and they were driven back with at least five killed and a large number wounded.[131]

Commandant General Brennan then ordered forward a storming party of twelve soldiers, led by Colonel David Reynolds and Captain Con O'Halloran, into the newly formed breach in the rear of the barracks. Hurling grenades before them, they were met by intense fire as they entered. Colonel Reynolds was severely wounded, while Captain Halloran was struck in the chest by a burst of Thompson submachine-gun fire. The storming party was driven back, with several dead on both sides. Many of the men in the barracks then retreated through the Red Cross hospital next door and escaped towards the Clare Hills, where they then joined up with Republicans in Clare.[132] It was now impossible for Connie and the remainder of his men to continue; they were surrounded, cut off from the rest of their comrades, outgunned and outnumbered. They had withstood everything that was thrown at them but realistically there was no point in continuing, as further resistance would have led to needless loss of life. To preserve the lives of his men, Connie decided to surrender.

All through the siege Connie was advising headquarters of his situation, as the Free State troops had not cut the telephone wires to the barracks, allowing him to communicate freely with them. When on the telephone advising them of his decision to surrender, the telephone earpiece was shot out of his hand by a Free State sniper, narrowly missing his head by centimeters. The Lee-Enfield .303 bullet was later made into a brooch and his girlfriend's name, 'S. Donnelly', was inscribed on it, as well as the date he was shot, 20 July. He must have kept it with him as a lucky charm throughout his time in prison, and it later became a treasured family keepsake.[133]

Some time later that evening, his gallant force of twenty-two remaining men reluctantly obeyed his last orders to destroy their arms, probably by bending the barrels or smashing their rifles to pieces. They then patiently awaited the arrival of Free State troops to take them into custody. The only type of white flag they had to indicate their surrender was an old flour bag, which was tied across a broom handle and pushed out the top right-hand window of the barracks. On the evening of 20 July, when Connie and his men surrendered, Commandant General Brennan was so impressed that he complimented Connie and his men on their magnificent defence. He also offered Connie a place on his staff as third in command, should he come over to the Free State side. Rather than sacrifice his principles and

Above left: The bullet that shot the telephone earpiece out of Connie's hand in the Strand Barracks.

Above right: The breach made in the rear of the Strand Barracks. (*Image kindly supplied by Limerick Museum.*)

Left: The breach made in the front of the Strand Barracks. (*Image kindly supplied by Limerick Museum.*)

Below: Connie with 1st Squadron Strand Barracks. Note the Captain's rank on his sleeve.

abandon his men, Connie refused and chose to be instead to be imprisoned with them.[134]

Phoblacht na hÉireann, on 3 August, reported, 'The courage, resource and endurance of all ranks of the Limerick Brigade won for them general admiration during the recent fighting particularly the splendid defence of the Strand and Castle Barracks against overwhelming odds.'

Imprisonment and the
end of the War

Connie and his men were then marched under armed escort from the Strand Barracks, across Sarsfield Bridge and on to William Street Barracks. The flour bag of surrender remained flying from the window of the Strand Barracks until sunset, when it was removed and retained by a Captain Hessian.

The Strand Barracks taken, the Free State troops then concentrated on the remaining three barracks. They moved the 18-pounder gun to fire on the Castle Barracks, which was set ablaze (though whether this was due to the shelling or the retreating garrison is unclear). The whole of the modern part was destroyed and only the Castle structure was left intact.[135]

A little after midnight, the Republican forces, in a convoy of cars, retreated along the Ballinacurra Road. The main body of them headed towards Kimallock, blocking roads with trees and mines, and blowing up bridges as they went. Intense rifle and machine-gun fire covered their retreat from O'Connell Avenue. At around 12.30a.m., there were two or three huge explosions in the New Barracks, caused by mines being detonated inside the gate leading to O'Connell Avenue. The explosions were so powerful that stones and debris were thrown into Wolfe Tone Street and other streets nearby, damaging the roofs and windows of some of the houses. The entire barracks complex, which covered fifteen to twenty acres, was completely burnt to the ground, but thankfully there were no casualties. The Ordnance Barracks was next to be set on fire. This, too, was completely destroyed. Patrick and the rest of the men in the Ordnance Barracks evacuated and they too headed

Castle Barracks on fire, 21 July 1922. (*Image kindly supplied by Limerick Museum.*)

Sarsfield Barracks ablaze, 21 July 1922. (*Image kindly supplied by Limerick Museum.*)

Looting at the Ordnance Barracks, 21 July 1922. (*Image kindly supplied by Limerick Museum.*)

towards Killmallock. The Fredrick Street Barracks (O'Curry Street) was set on fire by the boys of Na Fianna Éireann, but these fires were put out by the local population, as the barracks was close to a local gasworks and electricity station. The damage to Limerick City was immense and repairs were undertaken almost immediately. The total cost of destruction was estimated to be around almost £250,000. On 17 August 1922, once repairs had been completed by the office of public works, to both the Strand Barracks and the New Barracks, the cost of repairs was £1,400 and £10,000 respectively.

The remainder of the Republican forces retreated south towards Mallow and Fermoy (where Lynch had moved his headquarters on 15 July).[136] The *Limerick Leader* of 23 July 1922, announced that Limerick's hospital records showed a casualty list of ninety-eight after the Republicans took over the city on 2 July. Of that number, fifteen were dead, including seven civilians. The wounded were mainly civilians. The report stated it was impossible to estimate the Republican dead and wounded, but put the figure killed during the conflict at thirty.

After a few days, Connie and his men were again marched under armed guard along Mulgrave Street, from William Street Barracks to Limerick Prison. While there, Connie was elected the prisoners' commanding officer. In early August, during his stay, he organised a hunger strike with the other prisoners, against the appalling conditions, which were not in keeping with their status as political prisoners. This, the first of his series of hunger strikes in Free State prisons, lasted for six days. When Limerick Prison was built, it was meant to hold 120 prisoners, but was now holding prisoners from the west and the south areas, and their numbers had swelled to

Limerick Prison
today.

700, sometimes with six to a cell. There were no proper toilet facilities, and some prisoners had to sleep in the corridors. The overcrowding and lack of proper medical supplies meant that there was a serious threat of a typhoid fever outbreak. Several cases of dysentery were reported. Skin diseases such as scabies were common among inmates. The overcrowding got so bad that prisoners were being released because there simply was no room for them in the prison.[137] During Connie's time there, he was regularly visited by his family, especially his stepmother Hanora, and sisters Mamie, Babe and Josie, who brought him parcels, food and much-needed support.

He was also visited regularly by his girlfriend, Sally Donnelly. Sally was also a Volunteer, assigned to one of the ten Limerick branches of Cumann na mBan. But apart from this fact nothing has been documented about her Volunteer service. What I am sure of, is that she provided invaluable assistance in the provision of intelligence, which helped Connie in many of his operations. My mother told me that Sally would get British soldiers drunk to make them talk. Although nothing is known of her activities in the Volunteer movement, her role was no less important. The gallant ladies of Cumann na mBan provided vital support for the Volunteers, and the majority of operations could not have been performed without their assistance.[138] They also provided invaluable aid for Republican Prisoners. The ladies of Cumman na mBan did all they could to support and assist the prisoners and to comfort their families, as the McNamara family found out during Connie's stays in prison.

While the Free State forces were engaged in clearing the western end of the 'Limerick– Waterford Line', progress was also being made on the eastern end. Shortly after becoming commander-in-chief on 13 July, Michael Collins outlined a plan for an attack on the city of Waterford. This looked very difficult, as the Republican areas of South Tipperary and Cork bordered it, and also, to occupy Waterford City the Free State forces had to cross the River Suir, a very difficult task. The attack on Waterford was to be led by the forces in Kilkenny under Commandant General John Prout.[139]

The Republican garrison, under Colonel Commandant Pax Whelan, included the Waterford Brigade and possibly elements from Kerry and the First Cork Brigade; a total of between 200 and 300 men. They occupied various positions, the most important of which were their headquarters in the Infantry Barracks, the Artillery Barracks, Ballybricken Prison, a number of hotels along the quays, and the post office. These latter positions covered the Suir River, some 250 yards wide. However, because the Republicans had chosen the waterfront as the city's principle line of defence, they failed to place any troops on Mount Misery, which provided a commanding view of Waterford from the north bank. When taken by the Free State troops, late in the afternoon of 18 July, this was where they placed their 18-pounder gun. At 10.40a.m. the following day, they commenced firing on key positions in the town.[140]

The cantilever bridge that spanned the river remained raised. In the evening of 19 July, under cover of darkness, a detachment of 100 troops under Captain Ned O'Brien went across the river in rowing boats, and took over buildings in the city as a bridgehead. Because of intermittent firing from the post office, they were prevented from reaching the mechanism of the bridge, until that position was shelled by the 18-pounder. The Free State troops then lowered the bridge, and the rest of their forces entered the city at around 5.00p.m. Colonel Commandant Whelan could see that his position was now hopeless and ordered the barracks to be set on fire and the majority of his garrison to abandon the city. Whelan left a rear guard in the city under the command of Captain Jerry Cronin, so that fighting within the city continued into the afternoon of Friday 21 July.[141]

In all, ten men were killed in the battle for Waterford. Commandant General Prout failed to take advantage of his victory by conducting a close pursuit of the retreating Republicans, much to the frustration of the GHQ. Nevertheless, on Monday 24 July, he began his advance on Liam Lynch's former headquarters in Clonmel. Commandant General Prout's operation was to coincide with an offensive from Kilkenny in the north by a force under Comdt Liam McCarthy. Although stiff resistance was encountered along the way, Carrick-on-Suir fell to Free State forces on Thursday 3 August and Clonmel was captured a week later.[142]

The relative ease with which Free State forces rolled up the 'Limerick–Waterford Line' from the east, however, was not mirrored in General O'Duffy's advance southwards from Limerick City. Commandant General Liam Deasy's Republican forces, which had withdrawn from Limerick, concentrated in the town of Kilmallock, the northern approach to which was guarded by the towns of Bruree to the west and Bruff to the east. They had established their headquarters in Ashill Towers, Killmallock. The area had immense strategic importance, as it controlled rail and road routes to Kerry and Cork from Limerick City. It was the barrier to a Pro-Treaty advance on Munster from the north. Here, more than anywhere else during the Irish Civil War, the opposing sides would hold something like clearly defined front lines; each side maintaining a string of outposts in villages and towns, at crossroads, and upon hillocks, with a 'no-man's land' varying in width, between a few 100 yards to one mile. The conflict's most intense two weeks of fighting occurred within the Kilmallock–Bruff–Bruree triangle.[143]

General O'Duffy drew up the plans for the advance on Kilmallock with the assistance of his second-in-command, Commandant General W.R.E. Murphy. Murphy had served as an acting Brigadier General in the British Army during the Great War and was now put in charge of executing operations against Kilmallock. Unfortunately for the Free State troops, his experiences in the trenches appear to have adversely shaped his approach to war. On Sunday 23 July, Free State forces, already in possession of the town of Bruff, began their advance on Kilmallock. Much to the disgust of his men, Murphy gave orders to dig trenches, and the battle lines then came to resemble those of the Great War.[144]

The Free State troops, most whom were new recruits, were at a disadvantage in facing some of the best and most experienced of the IRA forces. General Eoin O'Duffy estimated that while his forces had about 1,300 rifles, the Republicans could muster over 2,000, and had 4 Lewis guns to his 1. Discipline was also a problem for O'Duffy, as many of his men deserted and joined the Republican side altogether, or simply ran away when they came under fire. It gave the men on the Republican side great heart to see the calibre of the men they were up against.[145] Bruree and Bruff were taken and retaken by one side and then another. Bruree was retaken by the Republicans on 24 July, and retaken by the Free State troops on 2 August. Bruff was retaken by the Republicans in a counter-attack on 23 July, and recaptured by the Free State troops on 30 July. With both towns now firmly in their control, the Free State concentrated all their attention on Killmallock.[146]

On 2 August 1922, Free State Army forces, under the command of General Paddy O'Daly, landed in Fenit, Co. Kerry, from the *Lady Wicklow*, with 500 troops. As a large part of the Republican garrison in Killmallock was made up of men from the Kerry Brigades, these were ordered to return to Kerry to block the advance of the Free State troops and to defend Tralee. The last linear defence of the Civil War in Munster by the Republican forces was in the Killmallock–Bruff–Bruree triangle, but this defence was now outflanked by the landing in Fenit. The priority was now for the Kerry Brigades to return and defend their homeland. The battle in Killmallock now became a rearguard action, covering the withdrawal of the Kerry troops. Their retreat was covered by the men of the Cork Brigades who fought with great courage and determination. While the seaborne landing in Fenit was the cause of the retreat, the overwhelming strength of the Free State

Forces would have led to it eventually. The landing and subsequent withdrawal also sounded the death knell of the Munster Republic. Killmallock was eventually captured on 5 August, by Free State troops.[147] This was probably where Patrick was captured and he was then taken to Limerick Prison to join his brother Connie.

On 7 August, the SS *Arvonia* and the SS *Lady Wicklow*, loaded with troops, armoured cars and 18-pounder guns, left Dublin docks. They avoided the block ships sunk by the Republicans on the channel leading into Cork (the capital of the Munster Republic), and made a surprise landing at Passage West near Spike Island, on Tuesday 8 August. Within three days, General Paddy O'Daly had taken control of the city. A huge convoy of lorries, with confused, demoralised Republicans, retreated westwards towards Macroom, burning barracks and destroying bridges as they went. The loss of Cork City was a major blow to the hopes of the Republicans and within days the towns of Macroom, Inchigeelagh, Bantry, Bandon and Clonakilty were occupied by the Free State. Fermoy, the last big town held by the Republicans, fell on 11 August, and General Liam Lynch was forced to move into the countryside. Republican operations then reverted to guerrilla warfare and sabotage.[148]

On 20 August, Michael Collins' convoy drove to Limerick from Dublin on his way to Beal na Blath.[149] The convoy arrived at Sarsfield Barracks at 2.35p.m. After discussions with military officers, Collins issued instructions that ciphers be sent to Dublin for the removal of 200 prisoners from Limerick Prison. He placed an order to supply 100 revolvers to General Eoin O'Duffy, and also made a request to the government to station Civic Guards in Limerick.[150] For some unstated reason he made

The SS *Arvonia* at Limerick docks. (Image kindly supplied by Limerick Museum.)

a request to make an ambulance available. Collins was later killed around 8.00p.m. on 22 August 1922 .[151] It is interesting to note that one of the last acts of his Collins' life was to organise the transfer of Connie and others from Limerick Prison.

On 28 August, in accordance with Collins' earlier instructions, the prisoners were removed from Limerick Prison and marched under armed guard to Limerick docks, where they were put aboard internment ship SS *Arvonia*, under the command of Commandant Frank Bolster (a member of Collins' squad). On their way, friends and relatives lined the streets and cheered them on. My mother related a story to my brother Tom; on their release from Limerick Prison, there was a huge reception committee for Connie and Patrick, made up of friends, family and well-wishers.

The upper deck of the ship housed around sixty Free

State troops, who were guarding the prisoners. There were about 600 prisoners in the lower cabin of the SS *Arvonia*, over which Connie was elected prisoners' commandant. The conditions aboard were appalling; the Free State troops closed the portholes, cutting off fresh air and ventilation. There was no bedding to sleep on, and there were no proper toilet facilities. There was no drinking water and the only rations the prisoners recieved was dry bread and tea twice a day. On 28 August, they sailed at half past four on the evening tide at a rate of seven knots. Because of her decrepid engines, age and condition, the SS *Arvonia* sailed close to the shore so that in case of emergency, she could be run aground on a convenient beach. They arrived at Dún Laoghaire port, Co. Dublin on 5 September, where they remained at anchor for around a week, while work on the facilities was being completed at Gormanstown camp. During that period, 170 more prisoners from Dundalk were placed on-board. The extra men now brought the total on the ship to around 770, adding to the already over-congested and deplorable conditions. About 100 of the men were badly seasick; they had to be taken ashore in launches and were released shortly afterwards. A hunger strike, lasting two days, was declared in protest, though given the meagre rations available, it really made little difference to the men.[152] However, there was a point to be made. When some prisoners started throwing lifebuoys overboard, one man was shot by the Free State troops.

Despite the vigilance of their escort, Connie staged a propaganda coup where, under the noses of the guards and the tight security, he established communications with Republican headquarters in Dublin. He did this by smuggling out a signed statement highlighting their plight, thus generating valuable publicity about the 'coffin ship'. Their story was published in the Republican newspaper *Phoblacht na hÉireann War News* on 9 September 1922, under the title 'Coffin Ship in Dublin Bay', which read:

> We have received from SS *Arvonia*, now at anchor in Dublin Bay guarded by a British man of war, a statement signed by Prison Comdt C. Mackey. On what Eamonn Roach TD describes as 'this coffin ship' are 550 Republican prisoners from Limerick Gaol. They have been housed in the lower cabin for five days and nights without ventilation (the portholes are kept closed), without exercise, without beds. There is no proper lavatory accommodation and for the insufficient lavatories there is no proper water supply. Among the prisoners are 50 Fianna boys aged 12 years upwards. Many of these have collapsed. There are wounded prisoners taken in action, whose wounds have not been dressed for ten days. The prisoners are starved, getting nothing but dry bread and tea twice a day. There is no drinking water. The ship is in the charge of Comdt F. Bolster who, when at Wellington Barracks, tortured every prisoner who passed through his hands. Bolster has already shot one prisoner on the *Arvonia*. What about Craig's prison ship now?

Finally, after eleven terrifying days, the poor prisoners disembarked SS *Arvonia* at Dún Laoghaire port. They were taken by train or lorry about twenty miles, through the villages of Swords and Balbriggan, to Gormanstown Camp. The prisoners arrived on 9 September 1922, and there they remained until November 1923. The prisoners' O/C was Oscar Traynor, who later went on to establish the Bureau of Military History, which documented the activities of the Volunteers from their inception to the Truce.[153]

28 September 1922: an Emergency Powers Bill was passed, empowering military courts with the right to impose the death penalty. It allowed a period of grace for any Republicans, caught with arms, to surrender. The law came into force on 15 October, and seventy-seven Republicans were executed (more than were executed by British authorities during the War of Independence, who executed twenty-five). This would lead both sides to commit atrocities that would generate long-lasting bitterness.[154] On 20 January 1923, Patrick Hennessy and Cornelius McMahon were executed in Limerick Prison, after they were captured under arms and having damaged the Ard Solus railway station near Quinn, Co. Clare.

A joint meeting of the Republican Government and the Army, held on 13-14 May 1923, instructed Frank Aiken, the Republican Commander, to cease fire and to dump arms. (Liam Lynch had been killed on 10 April, on the slopes of Knockmealdown Mountains Co. Tipperary.) The order was published on 24 May, on the same day de Valera released a proclamation to the Army, which declared, 'Further sacrifice on your part would now be in vain, and continuance of the struggle in arms unwise in the national interest. Military victory must now be allowed to rest for the moment with those who have destroyed the Republic.'[155] The Free State then concentrated on rounding up what was left of the Republican leadership and finding their hidden arms dumps, so the conflict would not be resumed at a later date.

Although the Civil War ended on 24 May 1923, the Free State continued to hold over 12,000 Republican prisoners in detention. They were, in effect, hostages, kept to prevent hostilities breaking out again. However, on 13 October 1923, a hunger strike started in Mountjoy Prison as a protest against the conditions and internment. Following the instructions of the camp councils, the strike soon spread to all prisons and internment camps, including Gormanstown, where Connie and Patrick were interned. At its height, there were around 8,000 Republican prisoners on hunger strike throughout the country.

When the strike reached Gormanstown, Oscar Traynor and his camp council organised the strike there. Connie went on hunger strike for a period of eleven days, before calling it off and starting to take food again. There are no records of Patrick having joined the strike, but he would probably have supported his brother on it. The strike was poorly organised; there was no clear direction of its purpose and no one knew when it was to be called off or by whom.

On 20 November, Commandant Denny Barry died in Newbridge Camp in Co. Kildare, and Andrew O'Sullivan died two days later in Mountjoy Prison. Both were from Cork. Many of those in various camps and prisons had broken off their strike and were taking food again. Eventually the strike was called off on 23 November, before any more deaths occurred. The Free State subsequently released the female Republican prisoners, but they released male prisoners in dribs and drabs, not wanting to release them all in one go, as they did not want to be seen to be influenced by the strike.[156] Patrick was released from Gormanstown in November. His pension application shows that his time in prison cost him upwards of £167 from his trade as a pork butcher. It does not state whether his release was before or after the strike ended. Most of the male Republicans were not released until the following year.

The Free State Government used the strike to pressurise Republican prisoners to sign the 'pledge' in order to gain their freedom. A few prominent strike leaders signed, and some were misled into doing so.[157] But the majority, like Connie, did not, even though they could have been released anytime by signing this pledge that they would not take up arms against the Free State Government. Connie and the majority of Republican prisoners chose to stay imprisoned and endure their hardships rather than by signing away their principles.

While Connie was interned in Gormanstown, he sang in the camp choir which comprised solely of Limerick men. The choir consisted of: Connie, his stepbrother Patrick, Patrick Kelleher, William Barry, Tom Martin, John Punch, Eamon Kelly, Aiden Muldowney, Rory Martin, Patrick Kane, Joseph

A page from the Gormanstown Camp diary, featuring the camp choir, entirely composed of Limerick men. The piece was kindly translated by Michael Kenny, of the National Museum of Ireland. The choir consisted of: Patrick Kelleher, William Barry, Patrick McNamara, Tom Martin, John Punch, Eamon Kelly, Aiden Muldowney, Rory Martin, Patrick Kane, Joseph Connolly, Michael Foley, David Sheriden, John Nolan, Tom Daly, Liam O'Kelly, Connie McNamara, John Hayes (Accompanist), and Dick MacDermot, LAA Choir Master.

Connolly, Michael Foley, David Sheriden, John Nolan, Tom Daly, Liam O'Kelly, John Hayes (Accompanist), and Dick Mac Dermot, LAA Choir Master.

In an autograph book, Connie preserved some illustrations, poems, familiar quotations, and reflections of fellow prisoners, as was the tradition of Republican internees in various prisons. On reading the Gormanstown autograph book, I was touched by the level of belief and commitment to the Republic the signatories had. One of the more remarkable lines in the autograph book is by prisoner J. O'Leary from Cork, who wrote, 'The slave who fights is a slave half free. But the willing slave is a slave indeed.'

Michael Kelly, of the National Museum of Ireland, has an extensive collection of autograph books from various camps and prisons of the period, and he described this as the only surviving book from Gormanstown that he has seen. While interned, Connie became friends with, among others, Sean T. O'Kelly (who later became President of Ireland), Oscar Traynor TD, and James Carroll, former Lord Mayor of Dublin. Connie remained there until November 1923, when he was transferred by lorry to Mountjoy Prison, on the north side of Dublin City. He was transported with Sean T. O'Kelly, Oscar Traynor and others, and he remained there until his release on 23 December 1923.[158]

IRPDF, Marriage and New York

On his release from prison, Connie became secretary of the
Limerick branch of the Irish Republican Prisoners' Dependents'
Fund (IRPDF) from 1924 to 1925. When the Truce was
declared on 11 July 1921, the IRPDF provided prisoners with
meals, shelter and sometimes even money, to buy clothes and
assist with fares home. During the War of Independence, the
IRPDF looked after prisoners returning from English prisons;
men often in a weakened state and in need of medical attention.
They also looked after the families of Volunteers killed by the
British, sometimes even paying the actual funeral costs.

Contrary to British actions during the War of Independence,
the Free State banned advertisements and public collections for
the fund during and after the Civil War. IRPDF offices were
raided and the staff arrested; funds were seized, as were clothes and
goods which had been collected. Funds, then, had to be collected
secretly, and around June 1923, there were 800-900 families in
Dublin who were receiving weekly grants. As Limerick was a
strongly Republican area, the numbers receiving grants would
also have been high. On a fundraising trip in America during that
period, the IRPDF aimed to raise at least £2,000 weekly from
America, but they admitted that it was woefully inadequate for
the number of families that they needed to look after.

Helping prisoners and their dependents was something
Connie felt strongly about. During his many incarcerations, he
had seen first-hand the hardships endured by prisoners' families
when their sole breadwinner was taken away from them. He
had also seen the comfort given to prisoners, knowing that their

families were financially cared for by the fund. But now it was Connie that was looking after ex-prisoners and their families, the victims of the Free State. As secretary of the Limerick branch of the fund, he was in charge of collecting monies and distributing aid to the needy Republican families of Limerick. He was in a very prominent position, but for all the wrong reasons.[159]

There was prolonged bitterness and animosity towards Republican ex-Volunteers after the war. Many were forced out of work and excluded from public office; considerable numbers were forced to emigrate. This, unfortunately, was also the case in Limerick City; in 1925 Connie had to step down as secretary of the IRPDF due to similar pressures. At the same time he was forced out of his job as a pork butcher and had to emigrate to America. This situation came about due to pressure from the Free State sympathisers (and possible work colleagues) who were resentful of his role on the Republican side in the Civil War. He feared for his life, which was very cheap in those days. There were plenty of cases of former Republicans being beaten up and even killed.[160] There were plenty of people around who would have liked to settle old scores. This is why he left his girlfriend Sally, and all his friends and family, and went to America in 1925. Like so many other Irishmen, he made his way to New York.

He and Sally took the train from Limerick to Cork and then travelled on to Cobh. When saying goodbye on the quayside of Cobh, Sally asked him to wait for her and to stay faithful; Connie promised her that he would. Connie sailed as a second-class passenger to New York. The crossing time would have been about six days, depending on the weather and seas. While he was in New York he worked in a dairy company called the Borden New York Condensed Milk Company. He became

Connie at an unidentified memorial.

firm friends with Tom Moakley, another ex-Volunteer from the Third Battalion (Castletownroche), Second Cork Brigade, and his sister May from Clenor, Doneraile, Co. Cork.[161] During his time in New York, Connie became very close to May but he honoured his commitment to his girlfriend Sally, and stayed faithful to her. There is no doubt that Connie fell in love with May in New York, but as he had given his word of honour, and was willing to forego his own happiness and selfish longings in order to stick to his principles.

During the IRA November Convention of 1925, Peadar O'Donnell moved a resolution to sever its connections with Sinn Féin and Dáil Éireann. It was passed with an overwhelming majority. Even though the IRA was now free of political control, many rank and file IRA members continued to have close links with de Valera and his inner circle. On 11 March 1926, Éamon de Valera, Connie's fellow Limerick man, resigned from the presidency of Sinn Féin and founded the 'Fianna Fáil' party (meaning 'Warriors of Destiny') on

23 March.[162] Because of its affinity with Republicanism, it later became known as the Republican Party and many IRA members joined it after it was formed. Connie later joined on his return to Ireland and became a staunch supporter of the party for life, like Patrick and Thomas.

It is not documented when Connie returned home, but it was probably around the time of his father Michael's death on 6 November 1928, or possibly earlier, in order to help out with the family. Michael McNamara died of cancer of the intestines and had been suffering for six months before he passed away. Connie returned to his family and long-time girlfriend Sally, but he also returned to the bitterness and animosity that forced him to leave Limerick in the first place. Those who had forced him away from everything he loved would not let him remain in Limerick long. Connie honoured his commitment to Sally Donnelly and they were married on 8 October 1929. Her family were originally from Fair Hill in Galway, and as was tradition at the time, they were married in the bride's parish, which was in St Patrick's Church, Forster Street, Galway. Connie's brother Thomas was his best man. The newlyweds then went to live in 1 Hassett Villas, Limerick City, next door to Sally's parents.

It did not take long after Connie's return to Limerick for the intimidation to start up again. He was victimised out of his job again and after only a few months of marriage, he was forced to emigrate to New York again in 1930. He left his pregnant wife Sally in the care of her parents, Jeremiah and Bridget Donnelly. In New York he resided in 3225 Shippet Villas, the Bronx. On this occasion he worked as a pork butcher in New York, rather than with his former company, Borden's, probably to avoid renewing his acquaintance with May. While Connie was in New York, his only daughter Patricia was born on 22 August 1930. While he was living in New York, he was offered a commission in the United States Army as a Colonel, which he declined. He had had seen enough of fighting during the troubles in Ireland.[163]

In his pension statement, Connie stated that he was forced to emigrate on two occasions, firstly in 1925 and then in 1930, after being victimised in his job as a pork butcher. It is safe to assume that he was working in one of the four large bacon factories, possibly Shaw's in Mulgrave Street, which was near his former home in Blackboy Pike. But it is hard to believe that a man who led an Active Service Unit of Irish Volunteers into conflict time and time again, a man who had seen and done terrible things, could be easily forced to leave his workplace, family and country. On condition of anonymity, the son of a Volunteer in 'A' Company related an account that his father told him of Connie shooting an informer in one of the side streets off the Abbey Bridge. If Connie personally executed someone, I have no doubt that he ordered his men to do similar tasks. So I have to ask myself, what could have happened to make a man like him leave his job, his loved ones and his country? The possibility exists that his life and lives of his family were in danger if he stayed in Limerick. There were many instances of ex-Anti-Treaty IRA Volunteers being beaten up and even killed. There were plenty of instances throughout the country of ex-Anti-Treaty IRA men being forced out of their jobs, homes and country. Unfortunately, similar incidents were happening in Limerick City. Because of his standing and prominence in the Republican forces during the Civil War, Connie was specially singled out, instead of his brothers Patrick and Thomas.

The Fianna Fáil party, under de Valera, won the general election of February 1932. This victory put Fianna Fáil in power and de Valera started to introduce policies and legislation that would

favour the Republican element. Thus the intimidation and vic-
timisation of Republicans started to ease and the tide started to
turn in their favor. The way was now open for Connie to return
to Limerick to his wife and daughter. Connie returned sometime
in 1934 to care for Sally, who was dying of TB, and his four-
year-old daughter, Patsy. He still found it difficult to find work
and applied for an IRA pension to help make ends meet. At the
time of his application, Connie was unemployed and not receiving any assistance, just living off his own resources.[164] So there
must still have been lingering resentment towards Republicans in
Limerick, which prevented him from finding work. Although he
had been forced to leave the country twice on threat of death on
account of his Republican status, Connie did not take an active
part in any of the subsequent IRA campaigns. Like the majority
of fellow Old IRA, he was anxious for peace.

Connie applied for an IRA pension on 19 January 1935, under
the Military Service Pensions Act, 1934. This piece of legislation
allowed the Anti-Treaty IRA who fought in the Civil War to
apply for a pension. Prior to that, the Army Pensions Act of 1923
only gave pensions to those who fought for the Free State Army.
At the time of his pension application, Connie was out of work.
Sally was entitled to claim for a War of Independence Medal and
a Volunteer pension, due to her activities in Cumann na mBan,
but she didn't apply for either, probably due to her TB. Patrick
applied for his pension on 5 June 1935, but for some strange
reason his application was rejected. Thomas McNamara never
applied for a pension, but eventually, in 1979, he applied for a War
of Independence Veterans' special allowance, which was granted
to him on 5 February 1980.

There were many Anti-Treaty IRA veterans who refused to
apply for pensions or medals; they did not want to apply to

a government that they saw as having betrayed the Republic they fought for. This is perhaps why Thomas did not apply for his pension and medal at the onset. His widow Elizabeth continued to receive his allowance after his death in 1990. In January 2000, to celebrate the new millenium, the Department of Defence wrote to all Veterans of the War of Independence and their spouses, to give them a one-off payment of £500 and an increase of 50 per cent in their pension.

Unfortunately Sally passed away on 22 June 1935. As there was growing tension in the Donnelly household, Connie left Hassets Villas and moved back into Blackboy Pike shortly after Sally died. This could have been due to the fact he had re-established contact with May, which the Donnellys may have seen as a slur on the memory of their daughter. He left his five-year-old daughter Patsy in the care of the Donnellys as he could not bring her to live in the already overcrowded two-bedroom McNamara house in Blackboy Pike.

Connie started work on 21 August 1935 for Limerick Corporation as a rent collection officer, exactly two months after Sally's death. After a three-week trial period he was of given an official letter of appointment by the Corporation on 18 September. He collected weekly rents on ninety-four houses in Thomondgate and also in the Prospect area near Sarsfield Barracks. His annual salary in 1935 was £495, 1s and 6d. This included bonuses of 11s per week and 1.25 per cent commission on the rent money he collected on those ninety-four houses. When the Central Statistics Office first started producing records in 1949, fourteen years later, the average annual wage of a clerk was £290. This indicates how well paid Connie was by the Corporation.[165]

Remarriage and Clenor

Shortly after Sally died, Connie wrote to May Moakley in New York, and proposed to her. She must have been in his thoughts since those days together in New York. May accepted and returned to Ireland as soon as she could, sailing from New York to Cobh and hence to her family home in Clenor, North Cork.[166] On 13 December 1935, Connie was finally granted an IRA pension, which allowed him six years and seven months service for pension purposes, providing him and his family with some financial security. The supporting statements were from his former brigade Commandant Peadar Dunne and his former Gormanston Camp Commandant Oscar Traynor.[167]

Connie and May were married in Annakissa church in Clenor on 18 February 1936, seven months after Sally's death. Because it happened so soon after Sally died, and being that it was his second marriage, Connie kept the wedding a very low-key affair. The general acceptance was for a widow or widower to wait at least two years after the death of their spouse before remarrying; to do otherwise was considered indecent. But nevertheless the timing of the wedding, so soon after Sally died, sent tongues wagging anyway. Connie was aged forty at the time and May was thirty-nine; perhaps if they wanted to start a family together they really couldn't afford to wait around for the traditional mourning period. The newly-weds rented a house from the Corporation in Clanmorris Avenue. Connie could have had a loan from the Corporation to purchase it outright, but being a private person, he did not want people to know his business and continued to rent it from them.[168] Sadly, this was a decision which was to have an adverse effect on May following his death.

Connie and his wife May, date unknown.

Connie's house in Clanmorris Ave, as it is today.

Tom Moakley, May's brother, returned to Clenor some time after the wedding to look after the family's eighty-acre dairy farm. His brother William, who had been left the farm, was in ill health and died later on 27 January 1937, leaving the farm to him. After they were married Connie and May spent their Christmases and a great deal of each summer with May's family in Clenor.[169]

After Sally's untimely death, Connie's daughter Patsy McNamara, was brought up in the Donnelly household and cared for by her grandparents, Bridget and Jeremiah. On 15 November 1938, Connie's mother-in-law Bridget Donnelly died of heart failure, brought on by bronchitis, and soon afterwards, Jeremiah brought Patsy to Connie's house in Clanmorris Avenue. Jeremiah was unable to look after her any more because he was dying of bronchitis himself. He passed away on 21 September 1939, due to heart failure, at his home in Hassett Villas, with Connie at his bedside. Whatever differences they had were put aside by that stage.

Connie worshipped Patsy and gave her the best education he could. He arranged for her to be educated in the Salesian

Primary School, around the corner from Clanmorris Avenue, on fashionable Shelbourne Road. When she was older, she went to the Presentation School in Sexton Street, as all the McNamaras did, and still do to this day. As an only child, she was given a lot of attention and lived in a much-protected way. Connie had a deep love for children and as his only surviving child; she was the apple of his eye.[170]

Michael Moakley, Tom's son, related to me stories of Connie, May and Patsy's visits to the Moakley family in Clenor. He remembered that Connie loved his fags and also liked to listen to a wind-up gramophone. Connie would bring records for the children to listen to, and also replacment needles for the gramophone. A record he was very fond of listening to was 'Little Brown Jug'. Connie used to cough badly at night and young Michael was worried that around Christmas time Connie's coughing would scare away Santa Claus. He also said that although Connie and his father, Tom Moakley, were

Connie's War of Independence Medal, with Comrac bar. The Comrac bar was awarded to Volunteers with actual active and armed service, such as the Active Service Units and Flying Columns.

both in the IRA, they never talked about it in front of them. Rather, if they needed to reminisce about those dark days, they told the children they were having a business meeting and the children knew enough to leave them alone.[171]

In 1940, a pregnant May was rushed to hospital in Limerick after she was bleeding quite badly. Unfortunately, she miscarried and was never able to have children after that. That must have been very difficult on the couple; for a man who loved children so much not to have a child with his wife must have been very hard indeed. Like her husband, May also had a great love of children, and this was shown every time she visited the Corbett house. Every time she came she would bring small gifts for the children and her serene aura brought peace and calmness to our house.[172]

On 21 January 1941, when the Irish Government introduced the War of Independence Medal, Connie received one with the Comrac bar. The Irish Government issued 15,224 medals with the Comrac bar, and 47,664 medals without it. But this was a small figure compared to the number of Volunteers who were active in the War of Independence.

Many Anti-Treaty veterans did not apply for either the pension or the medal as a matter of principle; they did not want to apply to a government whom they believed abandoned the Republic. The Department of Defence issued a press statement on 29 June 1942, stating that participants in the War of Independence who had been awarded Military Service pensions would be issued automatically with War of Independence Medals. Because of that, Connie's medal was granted automatically. Patrick, on the other hand, because his pension was rejected, applied for his medal on 27 August 1940, and his application for a War of Independence Medal was granted. His

Connie talking to a
Church of Ireland vicar.

supporting statements were from Connie, the Lord Mayor of
Limerick Dan Bourke, Davy Dundon and Michael Hartney,
who would himself become Mayor of Limerick in 1945.
Thomas, for some strange reason, left it until 14 October 1970
to apply for his medal. Initally it was rejected, as his membership as a Volunteer could not be verified by supporting statements; his former commanding officers were deceased or did
not contact the Department of Defence. Subsequently, on 21
October 1974, Michael Ryan, the honorary secretary of the
Mid-Limerick Brigade, interceded and they provided a supporting statement from Patrick Byrnes. Finally, on 2 January
1975, a War of Independence Medal was awarded to Thomas,
and on 28 April 1981, the Truce Commemoration Medal was
awarded to him as well. This medal was issued to Veterans who
were alive on 11 July 1971, to commemorate the fiftieth anniversary of the signing of the Anglo Irish Treaty.[173]

Connie was a devout Catholic and regularly served mass
at St Munchin's church, Limerick City, right up to later life,
whenever there was a shortage of servers. He also went to the
weekly Confraternity in the Redemptorist Church. When

Right: Connie and his daughter Patricia on her wedding day.

Below: The Wedding of Thomas Corbett and Patricia McNamara on 15 October 1952. From left to right: best man Thomas Larkin, a boyhood friend my father's who also served in the army with him; maid of honour, Noreen Ahern; Michael Corbett and Kathleen Moakley; Paddy Corbett; two unidentified girls, both Patsy's friends; Connie and his second wife May McNamara (*née* Moakley), and Nora Corbett (*née* Brassil) whose husband Patrick passed away in 1945.

staying in Clenor, he would stop to say a quick prayer every time he would pass the holy tree and the well of St Crannacht, close to the house. Like most people of that era, Connie went everywhere by bike, and was a well-known figure, cycling around Limerick in his cape in the rain.[174]

He was a strict teetotaller but he had a weakness for cigarettes and developed a very bad smoker's cough, which kept him (and those within earshot of him) awake at night in his later years. Every summer and Christmas, Connie, May and Patsy, visited the Moakley family in Clenor. They would get the bus from Limerick to Mallow, and then get a taxi from there to Clenor. In summertime, they would take the train from Ballyhooley to Tramore, and spend a week by the seaside. Michael Moakley remembered Connie's visits with fondness as he would always bring small gifts for the children and take them for walks in the countryside. Sometimes he would entertain them by climbing trees and on the way back to the farmhouse he would stop and pick flowers for May, especially primroses, which she was very fond of.

On 15 October 1952, in St Munchin's church in Clancy's Strand, Connie had the privilege of seeing his daughter Patsy marry Thomas Corbett, of 8 Sydenham Terrace, Ballincurra, Limerick. The church was only a few hundred yards from where, thirty years earlier, he had fought for his life in the Strand Barracks. This was the church where the deceased would have been brought after those terrible days. Now, there he was proudly giving his daughter away in marriage. Afterwards, they had the reception in the Ardhu Ryan Hotel, on the Ennis Road, now called the Clarion Suites.

Around October 1950, Noreen Murphy (*née* Ahern), who was Patsy's chief bridesmaid at her wedding in 1952, went to

Connie in his back garden in
Clanmorris Ave., 1946.

live with Connie and his family at Clanmorris Avenue. She
moved from Clenor, Doneraile, to attend secondary school in
the Presentation in Sexton Street, Limerick, but had to return
when her own mother took seriously ill in June, 1951. She
described Connie as a warm and welcoming man who made
her feel very much at home and part of the family during
her stay.[175]

One Christmas in the early fifties, there was an ill-fated trip
to see the Moakleys. Connie had recently learned to drive and
so he hired a car to drive May and Patsy to the Moakley home.
Driving through the narrow country lanes very close to Clenor,
he lost the brakes and drove into a flooded road and into a ditch.
They were all unharmed but all got the fright of their lives. They
were so badly affected, they returned immediately to Limerick
by bus, not even bothering to see the Moakleys.[176] Connie was
so badly affected by this incident he never drove again; after all,
he was in his mid-fifties when he learned to drive.

Funeral and Firing Party

Connie suffered a heart attack on Sunday 8 December 1957, and he died a week later at home in Clanmorris Avenue with his wife May by his side. As there was no telephone in the house, friends and relatives were told the sad news by word of mouth and also by telegram. Frank Thompson, of Thompson's Funeral Home, in Thomas Street was contacted by May and they made all the funeral arrangements; including the death notice in the *Limerick Chronicle* and the removal and burial services. Patrick, Thomas and other surviving members of the Mid-Limerick Brigade also assisted, by arranging the wording for his obituary and his headstone. They sent May a letter of condolence, expressing their sympathy for her loss on behalf of the brigade. The undertakers contacted Lieutenant Colonel J. Healy, Commanding Officer of the Twelfth Infantry Battalion in Sarsfield Barracks, who arranged a firing party of a NCO and six men, and a bearer party to lower the coffin into the grave.

The next day, Connie's remains were removed from his home in a horse-drawn hearse, along the Ennis Road, by Clancy's Strand to St Munchin's church. Later, Monsignor Michael Maloney recited evening prayers. People from all over Limerick and the surrounding counties attended the removal. The following day, the funeral made its way from the church in a black horse-drawn hearse covered in wreaths, and his flag-draped coffin was borne by surviving members of his battalion, probably including his stepbrothers Patrick and Thomas. They went down Clancy's Strand, past the Strand

Barracks, where he had fought so gallantly, over Sarsfield Bridge, along Mulgrave Street, past his old home in Blackboy Pike, to Mount St Lawrence Cemetery.

When the cortège arrived, the firing party of the Twelfth Infantry Battalion were at the graveside. Connie was buried with full military honours. His family, including his grieving widow May and daughter Patsy, former Volunteers from both sides of the Civil War, and many local dignitaries were present to pay their respects. Forty years previously, Connie was organising firing parties in this very same cemetery, and now the men of Twelfth Infantry Battalion were providing his firing party for him, just as he had in the past trained his men to do. Fr Maloney gave the graveside oration and the coffin was lowered into the grave by the bearer party. Afterwards, the firing party responded to their NCO's commands in Irish (*Lódáil, Tairgig, Lámhach*) and fired their salute, followed by the bugler, who sounded the last post. The process has remained unchanged from Connie's time up to this day. All Irish Army commands are still given in Irish, just like in the Volunteer days.

Before his coffin was lowered into the grave, the bearer party removed and neatly folded the flag from his coffin. The NCO in command presented his daughter Patsy with the tricolour, which had been draped on his casket. Unusually, she was allowed to keep it, as normally it was presented as a token to the widow and later returned to the presenting NCO. The fact Patsy was allowed to keep the flag reflected the esteem Connie was held in.

His obituary appeared on the back page of the *Limerick Chronicle* that same day, Tuesday 17 Dec 1957, and it read:

DEATH OF GALLANT IRISHMAN

Widespread regret was expressed at the death of Mr Cornelius McNamara, 'St Annes', Clanmorris Avenue, Ennis Road, which occurred on Sunday. Mr McNamara, who was an official of Limerick Corporation, had been carrying out his duties up to very recently and few of his friends were aware of him being ill. When the 2nd Battalion of the IRA was organised in Limerick, he was one of the first to join and gave outstanding service during the War of Independence. So highly were his services rated, that soon he was promoted to the rank of Lieutenant and later became captain of the Company. He served terms of imprisonment in Irish and English prisons and, when released after the Treaty, attached himself to the Republician Party. During the Civil War, he was officer commanding the Strand Barrack, which was being held by Republican troops. Captain McNamara was called upon to surrender but refused to do so, holding the barracks until it was shelled from an 18-pound artillery piece. When he eventually had to surrender, he was complimented by the Free State officer in charge on the magnificent defence he put up, he was arrested and interned and released late in 1923. While interned he was a very intimate friend of Mr Sean T. O'Kelly President of Ireland and the present Lord Mayor of Dublin.

There is no doubt that Connie was a hero, a natural leader and a man guided by principle and conviction. But he was much more then the gallant warrior and enduring prisoner. Connie had a romantic side to him and loved the women in his life very much. He also had very evident love of children, as shown to his daughter Patsy, and also to the Moakley children. It probably saddened him deeply that he was not to have children with May.

Connie in his back garden in Clanmorris Ave., date unknown.

Connie was a man guided by principle, a man who never took the easy way out, even when the right way was fraught with danger and difficulty; a man who lived by a moral code and stuck to it in spite of whatever hardships or difficulties he had to face. No matter who he met, Connie Mackey made an impression, and left them holding a deep admiration and respect for him. Connie is an example to all of us, that a man of humble origins can achieve great things.

Bibliography

UNPUBLISHED WORKS

British National Archive file: WO/73/116
British National Archive file: WO/35/127
British National Archive file: WO 78/3181 (Map of Strand Barracks)
Connie McNamara, application for IRA Pension:
 Application MSP34/1
 Referee's decision MSP34/2
The Department of the Taoiseach ('Irish Soldiers in the First World War')
Irish Republican Constitution, IRB Supreme Council
Irish Statute Book, Acts of the Oireachtas, Emergency Powers Act, 1945
Irish Statute Book, Acts of the Oireachtas, Emergency Powers Act, 1976
Limerick City Battalion IRA Roll
National Archives of Ireland, File Reference FIN 1/1827
Patrick McNamara, application for IRA Pension:
 Application MSP34/1
 Referee's decision MSP34/2
Patrick McNamara, application for a War of Independence Medal: 12813/B2
Republican autograph book from Gormanstown camp, 1922-1923
Thomas McNamara, application for a Special allowance
Thomas McNamara, application for a War of Independence Medal: 12813/B2
Witness Statement 1423, Jeremiah Cronin
Witness Statement 1710, Liam Forde
Witness Statement, Limerick City First Battalion Committee John Larkin
    (Secretary) and Chairman, Patrick Foley

ARCHIVES

Army Archives, Dublin
Central Dublin Library
Cork Central Library
Cork Public Museum
Department of Defence, Dublin
Ellis Island Archives, New York
Franklin D. Roosevelt Presidential Library and Museum, New York
Inland Revenue, Ireland
Irish Bureau of Military History

Kerry County Library
Limerick City Council Records
Limerick City Library
Limerick Museum
Limerick Registry Office
Kilmainham Museum, Dublin
Mount St Lawrence Cemetery, Limerick City
National Archives of Great Britain, Kew
National Archives, New York
National Archives and Records Administration's Northeast Regional Archives,
    New York City
National Archives and Records Administration, Washington DC
National Library of Ireland
National Museum of Ireland
National Photographic Archives of Ireland
New York Public Library
Parliamentary Archives of the House of Commons, London
Peace Commissioner Unit, Department of Justice
Thurles Library

PUBLISHED WORKS

Bennett, Richard, *The Black and Tans* (Barnes and Noble: New York, 1995).
Cahill, Liam, *Forgotten Revolution: Limerick Soviet, 1919 – A Threat to British Power*
    (O'Brien Press: Dublin, 1990).
Coogan, Tim Pat, *1916: The Easter Rising* (Phoenix: London, 2005).
Coogan, Tim Pat, *De Valera: Long Fellow, Long Shadow* (Arrow Books: London,
    1995).
Coogan, Tim Pat, *The Man who made Ireland: The Life and Death of Michael Collins*
    (Palgrave: New York, 1990).
The 1966 Limerick Commemoration Committee, *Cuimhnionn Luimneach*
    ('Limerick Remembered').
Curran, Joseph M., *The Birth of the Irish Free State 1921-1923* (University of Alabama
    Press: Alabama, 1980).
Dwyer, Ryle T., *Tans, Terror & Troubles: Kerry's Real Fighting Story 1913-1923*
    (Mercier: London, 2001).
Ebenezer, Lyn, *Fron-Goch and the Birth of the IRA*, (Gwasg Carreg Gwalch: Wales,
    2005).
Handbook for Volunteers of the Irish Republican Army (Paladin Press: Colorado, 1985).
Harnett, Mossie, *Victory and Woe* (University College Dublin Press: Dublin, 2002).
Hart, Peter, *Mick: The Real Michael Collins* (Pan Books: London, 2006).
Harrington, Niall C., *Kerry Landing August 1922 an episode of the Civil War* (Anvil
    Books: Dublin, 1992).
Hopkinson, Michael, *Green against Green, The Story of the Irish Civil War* (Gill &

Macmillan: Dublin, 2004).

Hopkinson, Michael, *The Irish War of Independence* (Gill & Macmillan: Dublin, 2002).

Limerick's Fighting Story, Anvil edition.

Limerick's Fighting Story, Kerryman edition.

Macardle, Dorothy, *The Irish Republic* (Irish Press Ltd: Dublin, 1951).

McCarty, Cal, *Cumann na mBann and the Irish Revolution* (Collins Press: Cork, 2007).

Neeson, Eoin, *The Civil War 1922-1923* (Poolbeg Press: Dublin, 1989).

O'Haicead, Padraig, *Keep Their Names Evergreen* (Padraig O'Haicead: Tipperary, 2003).

O'Donoghue, Florence, *No Other Law* (Irish Press Ltd: Dublin, 1954).

O'Mahony, Edward, *Michael Collins: his life and times* (Edward O'Mahony, 1996).

O'Malley, Ernie, *On Another Man's Wound* (Roberts Rinehart Publishers: Colorado, 1999).

O'Malley, Ernie, *The Singing Flame* (Anvil Books: Dublin, 1992).

O'Neill, Tom, *The Battle of Clonmult* (Nonsuch Publishing: Dublin, 2006).

Redmond, Adrian, *That Was Then, This Is Now: Change in Ireland 1949-1999* (The Stationery Press: Dublin, 2000).

White, Q., & O'Shea, B., *Irish Volunteer Soldier 1913-1923* (Osprey Publishing: Oxford, 2003).

Younger, Calton, *Ireland's Civil War* (Fontana Press: London, 1986).

NEWSPAPERS AND PERIODICALS

The Capuchin Annual
IRA Daily Bulletin
The *Irish Independent*
The Irish Times
Limerick Chronicle
Limerick Leader
Murroe/Boher Christmas Newsletter 1995
Nenagh Guardian
The New York Times
The Old Limerick Journal
An Phoblacht War News
Tipperary Star

TELEVISION AND CINEMA

Michael Collins, 1996
The Wind That Shakes the Barley, 2006

Endnotes

1916: THE EASTER RISING

1. Connie McNamara, IRA Pension application MSP34/1.
2. Hopkinson,M., *The Irish War of Independence* (Gill & Macmillan: Dublin, 2002), p.11.
3. *Cuimhnionn Luimneach*, p.15 and Witness Statement 1710 of Liam Forde.
4. Coogan,T.P., *1916: The Easter Rising* (Phoenix: London, 2005), p.59.
5. *Cuimhnionn Luimneach*, p.15, and Witness Statement 1710, Liam Forde.
6. Ibid. p.17, and Witness Statement 1710.
7. *Limerick's Fighting Story* (Kerryman edition), p.201, and McCarthy,C. *Cumann na mBann and the Irish Revolution* (Collins Press: Cork, 2007), p.34.
8. *Cuimhnionn Luimneach*, p.19, *Limerick's Fighting Story* (Anvil Edition) p.31.
9. *Cuimhnionn Luimneach*, p.21.
10. Ibid.
11. Ibid., and Coogan, *1916: The Easter Rising,* p.86.
12. Ibid.
13. *Cuimhnionn Luimneach*, p.23.
14. Ibid p.25.
15. Ibid p.27.
16. Ibid.
17. Ibid p.29, and Coogan, *1916: The Easter Rising*, p.89.
18. *Cuimhnionn Luimneach*, p.29, and *Limerick's Fighting Story* (Anvil), p.34.
19. Ibid., and Coogan, *1916: The Easter Rising*, p.90.
20. Ibid. p.31, and Witness Statement 1710, and *Limerick's Fighting Story* (Anvil) p.34.
21. *Cuimhnionn Luimneach*, p.33, and Witness Statement 1710, and *Limerick's Fighting Story* (Anvil), p.35.
22. Ibid.
23. Ibid. p.35 and Witness Statement 1710, and *Limerick's Fighting Story* (Anvil), p.36.
24. Witness Statement Limerick City First Battalion Committee John Larkin (Secretary) and Chairman Patrick Foley.
25. *Cuimhnionn Luimneach*, p.41, and Witness Statement 1710, and *Limerick's Fighting Story* (Anvil), p.38.

1917: THE SECOND BATTALION AND THE IRB

[26] Connie McNamara, MSP34/1, and Witness Statement 1710.

[27] *Limerick's fighting Story* (Kerryman) p.74.

[28] Connie McNamara, MSP34/1.

[29] Ibid.

[30] Ibid.

[31] IRB Supreme Council, *Irish Republican Constitution*, p.3.

[32] Connie McNamara, MSP34/1.

[33] *Irish Republican Constitution* p.2.

1918: PROMOTION AND THE CONSCRIPTION CRISIS

[34] Connie McNamara, MSP34/1.

[35] Patrick McNamara, IRA Pension application, MSP34/1.

[36] Thomas McNamara, Special Allowance application, told to author by his daughter Maura.

[37] Hopkinson, *The Irish War of Independence*, p.17, and Coogan, T.P., *The Man who made Ireland: The Life and Death of Michael Collins* (Palgrave: New York, 1990), p.88, and Limerick City Battalion IRA Roll, p.10.

[38] The Department of the Taoiseach ('Irish Soldiers in the First World War').

[39] *Limerick's Fighting Story* (Kerryman), p.203, and McCarthy, p.142, and Witness Statement 1710.

[40] Witness Statement 1710.

[41] *Limerick's Fighting Story* (Anvil) p.176.

[42] Connie McNamara, MSP34/1.

[43] Ibid.

1919: THE WAR OF INDEPENDENCE AND ROBERT BYRNE

[44] Coogan, *The Man who made Ireland*, p.105, and Hopkinson, *The Irish War of Independence*, p.115.

[45] Connie McNamara, MSP34/1.

[46] Ernie O'Malley, *On Another Man's Wound* (Roberts Rinehart Publishers: Colorado, 1999), p.210.

[47] Connie McNamara, MSP34/1.

[48] D.O.R.A. The Defence of the Realm Act 1914 was passed in the UK on 8 August 1914, during the early weeks of the First World War. It gave the British Government wide-ranging powers during the First World War years and beyond. The legislation gave the government executive powers to suppress published criticism, imprison without trial and to commandeer economic resources for the war effort. Although the act was introduced to control resources for the war effort, it was mainly used during the War of Independence for the arresting of political prisoners.

49 Liam Cahill, *Forgotten Revolution: Limerick Soviet, 1919 – A Threat to British Power* (O'Brien Press: Dublin, 1990), p.45.

50 Limerick Workhouse or The Union Infirmary, situated on Shelbourne Road, was built in 1841 for the poor of Co. Limerick and Co. Clare. It is now called St Camillus' Hospital and amongst other services housed there is the Registrar's office.

51 Cahill, p.49, and *Limerick's Fighting Story* (Anvil), p.179.

52 Ibid., and Connie McNamara, MSP34/1, and Patrick McNamara, MSP34/1.

53 Ibid, p.49, and *Limerick's Fighting Story* (Anvil), p.181.

54 Ibid. p.50, *Limerick's Fighting Story* (Anvil), p.181, and told to author by Paddy McNamara.

55 *Limerick's Fighting Story*, (Anvil) p.185, and *Limerick Chronicle* (10 April 1919).

56 Patrick McNamara, MSP34/1.

57 Cahill, p.54, and *Limerick's Fighting Story* (Anvil), p.184, and *Limerick Chronicle* (10 April 1919).

58 Mount St Lawrence cemetery is situated in Mulgrave Street, on the south side of Limerick, and where records date back to 1855. An extension to this cemetery was opened in 1960. There are twenty-one brave volunteers buried in the Republican plot, including the Manchester Martyrs, Robert Byrne, the murdered Mayors of Limerick George Clancy and Michael O'Callaghan, Thomas McInerney, (with whom Connie was incarcerated), Sean Wall (Brigadier of the East Limerick Brigade), and Sean South. There are many other Republican graves in the cemetery including those of Cornelius McNamara and his stepbrother Patrick.
The Limerick Republican Graves Association maintains these Republican graves. This is a regional offshoot of the National Graves Association, which maintains Republican graves and memorials throughout Ireland.

59 Connie McNamara, MSP34/1, Patrick McNamara, MSP34/1.

60 Connie McNamara, MSP34/1.

61 As told to author by Michael Moakley, May McNamara's nephew.

62 Connie McNamara, MSP34/1.

63 *Limerick's Fighting Story* (Anvil) p.157, and Limerick City Battalion IRA Roll, p.10.

1920: THE ACTIVE SERVICE UNIT

64 Connie McNamara, MSP34/1.

65 Ibid., and *Limerick Leader* (26 January 1920), and Murroe/Boher Christmas Newsletter, 1995, p.49-50.

66 *Limerick Leader* (26 January 1920, 29 March 1920 and 6 September 1920).

67 Connie McNamara, MSP34/1, and *Limerick Leader* (8 March 1920).

68 Connie McNamara, MSP34/1, *Limerick's Fighting Story* (Anvil), p.158, and *Limerick Chronicle* (9 November 1920).

[69] Ibid., and *Limerick Chronicle* (8 May 1920).

[70] Ibid., and *Limerick's Fighting Story* (Anvil), p.79.

[71] Ibid.

[72] O'Haicead, Padraig, *Keep Their Names Evergreen* (Padraig O'Haicead: Tipperary, 2003), p.125-130, and *Neanagh Guardian* (17 July 1920), and O'Malley, *On Another Man's Wound*, p.198-200.

[73] Connie McNamara, MSP34/1, *Limerick Leader* (17 September 1920), and Coogan, *The Man who made Ireland*, p.183.

[74] *Limerick's Fighting Story* (Kerryman), p.201, and McCarthy, p.129.

[75] *Limerick's Fighting Story* (Anvil), p.85-87.

[76] British National Archive file WO/73/116.

[77] *Limerick Leader* (13 August 1920), and Coogan, *The Man who made Ireland*, p.155.

[78] Connie McNamara MSP34/1, and *Limerick Leader* (17 September 1920).

[79] Hopkinson, *The Irish War of Independence*, p.93.

[80] Connie McNamara, MSP34/1.

[81] Irish Republican Police (IRP). The IRP was founded between April and June 1920. It was raised by the IRA chief of staff and Cathal Brugha, Minister for Defence, and then handed over to the Minister for Home Affairs of Dáil Éireann. The purpose of the IRP was to provide security for the Republican Courts, as well as to enforce their decrees. They generally came from the ranks of the IRA. The IRP operated according to the IRA brigade structures and each brigade police unit was headed by a brigade police officer. The members of the IRP wore no uniform; however some units wore armbands with the letters IRP. It was replaced in February 1922 by the Civic Guard.

1921: THE TRUCE

[82] *Limerick's Fighting Story*, (Anvil) p.120.

[83] *Limerick's Fighting Story*, (Anvil) p.120-128, and Patrick McNamara, MSP34/1.

[84] Limerick City Battalion IRA Roll, p.10.

[85] Spike Island (Fort Westmoreland) is situated in the mouth of Cork Harbour. Records show that this was first used as a fort from c.1779, and in 1790 was named Fort Westmorland after the Earl of Westmorland, the Lord Lieutenant of Ireland. In 1845 Spike Island was selected as a male convict prison. It housed prisoners right up to 1994. By a clause in the 1921 Anglo-Irish Treaty the harbour defences at Cork, Berehaven and Lough Swilly were to remain under the control of British Government and were known as the 'Treaty Ports'. In 1938, the harbour defences were taken over by the Irish Government, and Fort Westmorland was renamed Fort Mitchell.

[86] Connie McNamara, MSP34/1.

[87] Witness Statment.1710, and Hopkinson, *The Irish War of Independence*, p.119.

[88] *Limerick's Fighting Story* (Anvil), p.193-199, and Patrick McNamara, MSP34/1.

[89] *Limerick's Fighting Story* (Anvil), p.167.

90 British National Archive file, WO/35/127.
91 Connie McNamara, MSP34/1.
92 Hopkinson, *The Irish War of Independence*, p.196, and Coogan, *The Man who made Ireland*, p.216.
93 Hart, P., *Mick: The Real Michael Collins* (Pan Books: London, 2006), p.291, and Coogan, *The Man who made Ireland*, p.234.
94 Connie McNamara, MSP34/1.
95 Younger, C., *Ireland's Civil War* (Fontana Press: London, 1986), p.242, and Harrington, N.C., *Kerry Landing August 1922 an episode of the Civil War* (Anvil: Dublin, 1992), p.8,10.
96 Connie McNamara, MSP34/1, and O'Malley, E., *The Singing Flame* (Anvil: Dublin, 1992), p.19-23.
97 *Limerick's Fighting Story* (Kerryman), p.204, and McCarthy, p.128, 145.
98 *Limerick's Fighting Story* (Kerryman), p.205, and McCarthy, p.202.

1922: THE CIVIL WAR

99 Younger, p.450, and Hopkinson, *Green against Green, The story of the Irish Civil War* (Gill & Macmillan: Dublin, 2004), p.189.
100 WO/35/127.
101 Younger, p.243, and Neeson, E. *The Civil War 1922-1923* (Poolbeg Press: Dublin, 1989), p.92.
102 Hopkinson, *Green against Green*, p.64.
103 Connie McNamara. MSP34/1, Thomas McNamara Special Allowance application.
104 The Strand Barracks dates from the eighteenth century and was built in 1774. It was a former workhouse called the House of Industry, built to help the destitute of Limerick City. It later became a British Army barracks during the nineteenth century, in order to protect both Wellesley (Sarsfield) Bridge and Thomand Bridge. The British handed the barracks over to the Free State in March 1922, who in turn handed it over to Republican forces. It was surrendered it to the Free State forces in July 1922 during the Civil War. The Free State closed the barracks and it was taken over by Limerick Corporation around 1935, becoming their works yard. Then it passed out of their hands in 1990, and it has now become the Castle Court complex of two-storey houses and apartments.
105 Connie McNamara, MSP34/1. Thomas McNamara Special Allowance application.
106 Neeson, p.103.
107 Coogan, *The Man who made Ireland*, p.363, and Hart, p.382.
108 Hopkinson, *Green against Green*, p.120, and Younger, p.324.
109 Hopkinson, *Green against Green*, p.147, and Younger, p.371.
110 Hopkinson, *Green against Green*, p127-129, and Younger, p.278.
111 Coogan, *The Man who made Ireland*, p.329.

[112] Younger, p.313.
[113] Ibid, p.373, and Hopkinson, *Green against Green*, p.147.
[114] Hopkinson, *Green against Green*, p.139.
[115] Hopkinson, *Green against Green*, p.149, and Younger, p.377.
[116] Neeson, p.145, and Younger, p.379.
[117] Hopkinson, *Green against Green*, p.150.
[118] Neeson, p.145, and Patrick McNamara, MSP34/1.

THE STRAND BARRACKS

[119] Younger, p.371.
[120] *The Old Limerick Journal* Winter Edition, 2002, p.19.
[121] Neeson, p.147, and Younger, p.380, and *The New York Times* (20 July 1922).
[122] Hopkinson, *Green against Green*, p.149.
[123] Neeson, p.147, and *Limerick Chronicle* (11 July 1922).
[124] *The Old Limerick Journal* Winter Edition, 2002, p.17.
[125] Connie McNamara, MSP34/1, and *Phoblacht na hEireann War News* No. 21 (22 July 1922).
[126] For some strange reason it became common practice for the Free State troops to name their armoured cars. Any armoured cars captured by Republican forces were quickly re-christened.
[127] Connie McNamara, MSP34/1.
[128] Connie McNamara, MSP34/1.
[129] Younger, p.381, and Neeson, p.148, and *The New York Times* (22 July 1922).
[130] Connie McNamara, MSP34/1.
[131] Younger, p.381, and Neeson, p.148.
[132] Ibid.
[133] As told to author by Patsy Corbett.
[134] *The Old Limerick Journal* Winter Edition, 2002, p.21, and Connie McNamara, MSP34/1, and Thomas McNamara, War of Independence Medal Application.

IMPRISONMENT AND THE END OF THE WAR

[135] *The Old Limerick Journal* Winter Edition, 2002, p.21 and National Archives of Ireland, File Reference FIN 1/1827.
[136] Neeson, p.149, and *Limerick Chronicle* (11 July 1922).
[137] Connie McNamara, MSP34/1, and Hopkinson, *Green against Green*, p.139.
[138] *Limerick's Fighting Story* (Kerryman), p.205.
[139] Hopkinson, *Green against Green*, p.153.
[140] Neeson, p.155.
[141] Hopkinson, *Green against Green*, p.155, and Younger, p.392.
[142] Hopkinson, *Green against Green* p157, and Younger, p.402.
[143] Hopkinson, *Green against Green*, p.150, and Younger, p.402.
[144] Younger, p.403.

[145] Hopkinson, *Green against Green*, p.151.

[146] Neeson, p.205.

[147] Ibid. p.209, and Hopkinson, *Green against Green*, p.152,166.

[148] Hopkinson, *Green against Green*, p.163, and Younger, p.408.

[149] Beal na Blath ('mouth of the flowers') is a village six miles outside Bandon, west Cork, near where Michael Collins was killed on 22 August 1922. The Fine Gael party hold an annual commemoration on the anniversary of his death.

[150] The Civic Guard was formed by the Provisional Government in February 1922 to take over the responsibility of policing the fledgling Irish Free State. It replaced the Royal Irish Constabulary and the Irish Republican Police. It was renamed the Garda Síochána after the creation of the Irish Free State on 8 August 1923 and remains the official police force of the Irish Republic to this day.

[151] O'Mahony, E., Michael Collins: his life and times, (Edward O'Mahony, 1996), p.10.

[152] Connie McNamara, MSP34/1 and *The Old Limerick Journal* Winter Edition, p.9.

[153] The Bureau of Military History 1913-1921, part of the Irish Military Achieves, was established in January 1947 by Oscar Traynor TD, http://www.military.ie/ images/padraig_pearse_letter.pdf Minister for Defence and Connie's former Commandant in Gormanstown. The objective of the Bureau was to assemble and co-ordinate material to form the basis for the compilation of the history of the Volunteers from its inception on 25 November 1913, to the Truce on 11 July 1921.

[154] Hopkinson, *Green against Green*, p.181.

[155] Younger, p.509.

[156] Connie McNamara, MSP34/1, and Hopkinson, *Green against Green*, p.268-270.

[157] Hopkinson, *Green against Green*, p.270.

[158] Gormanstown Camp autograph book, and Connie McNamara, MSP34/1.

IRPDF, MARRIAGE AND NEW YORK

[159] Connie McNamara, MSP34/1, and IRA Daily Bulletin No. 214 (8 June 1923).

[160] Connie McNamara, MSP34/1, and Younger, p.509, and Hopkinson, *Green against Green*, p.274.

[161] Told to author by Mike Moakley, May's nephew.

[162] Coogan, T.P., *De Valera: Long Fellow, Long Shadow* (Arrow Books: London, 1995), p.384.

[163] Told to author by Patsy Corbett.

[164] Connie McNamara, MSP34/1.

[165] Limerick Corporation archive records, and Redmond, A. *That Was Then, This Is Now: Change in Ireland 1949-1999* (The Stationery Press: Dublin, 200), p.137.

REMARRIAGE AND CLENOR

166   Told to author by Mike Moakley.
167   Connie McNamara, IRA Pension application, referee's decision, MSP34/2.
168   Told to author by Mike Moakley.
169   Told to author by Mike Moakley.
170   Told to author by Noreen Murphy.
171   Told to author by Mike Moakley.
172   Told to author by Mike Moakley and Neil Corbett.
173   www.irishmedals.com, and Patrick McNamara, MSP34/1, and Thomas McNamara War of Independence Medal application.
174   Told to author by Mike Moakley.
175   Told to author by Noreen Murphy.
176   Told to author by my brother Tom Corbett.

Index